AROUND THE WORLD IN 80 CIGARS

THE TRAVELS OF AN EPICURE

Nick Hammond.

July '20.

AROUND THE WORLD IN 80 CIGARS

THE TRAVELS OF AN EPICURE

Nick Hammond

Red Door

Published by RedDoor
www.reddoorpress.co.uk

ISBN 978-1-910453-68-1

A CIP catalogue record for this book is available
from the British Library

Cover design: Simon Avery

Illustrations: Sam Bridge

Internal design & typesetting: Westchester Publishing
Services

Print and production handled by Jellyfish Solutions Ltd

To my girls

Contents

Foreword

We were more than happy when Nick asked if we'd be willing to provide a foreword to his forthcoming book. We've known Nick for many years and always been appreciative of the time, thought and creativity he offers those of us in the cigar industry. The way he writes is so different – colourful, evocative and with a style that is unmistakably his. Nick's originality has now conjured something truly unique for your reading pleasure: *Around The World in 80 Cigars: The Travels Of An Epicure*.

Each chapter is irreverent, educational and laugh out loud funny. Nick has found a way to weave cigars into the stories without detracting from the action or indeed from the humour. It's a brilliant read and an inspiration to get out and see the world – with a good cigar, of course.

Congratulations, Nick, on this triumph. And we look forward to more adventures with you, home and abroad.

– Edward and Eddie Sahakian,
Davidoff of London, March 2019

CHAPTER ONE

Moustache

NO LILY-HANDED BARONET HE, A GREAT BROAD-SHOULDERED
ENGLISHMAN, A LORD OF FAT PRIZE-OXEN AND OF SHEEP,
A RAISER OF HUGE MELONS AND OF PINE.

— Tennyson

The hairy guy leering in my direction wears a fez and a moustache in which well-to-do blackbirds could happily retire.

He's pointing first at me and then at the television dangling precariously in the corner of the room. I can't make my mind up whether it's because he's friendly – or because he's considering dragging me out back to do unspeakable things to me.

Either way, it's intimidating and I'm not quite sure how to react.

I cough, manage a weak smile and give him a nervous nod. I only came in here for a cigar.

I look back longingly at the door to the outside world, but don't want to appear rude. The hairy guy's moustache parts to reveal a picket fence of teeth – and he starts to point with more urgency. What seems to be exercising him is the live Arabic footage being screened in grainy images in the corner of this little Tunisian café, where dust motes dance through shafts of sunlight and the air is thick with the heavy scent of last night's *shisha* pipe.

The TV reception is poor, the camerawork erratic and the copious subtitles in Arabic; but I have a sneaking suspicion of what he's getting at, pointing repeatedly to the little telly in the corner.

You see, thoughts of forthcoming public interactions like this have been bubbling away in the back of my mind since I arrived in Tunisia in a dusty whirl of grit, heat and a surfeit of poor-quality airline gin and tonic.

I've managed, in typically inept fashion, to coincide my arrival with the outbreak of the latest episode of the Iraq War saga. In a bout of ill-advised sangfroid, I booked my tickets while international posturing was reaching handbags-at-dawn stage, and when I left the UK at some ungodly hour this morning, several recently dug-up 'experts' were opining that military intervention was becoming increasingly likely.

Turns out they were right – and I'd made a mistake.

Now I wasn't flying to Iraq, of course, but Tunisia is a devoutly Muslim country and I had wondered how I might be received.

My carefree attitude was reduced in careful stages throughout transit until, barely through the sweat-inducing grilling I'd been given at Tunis Immigrations and the bone-jarring transportation on to my hotel accommodation, I noticed the television set in the lobby showing unmistakeable pan shots of desert; some bored soldiers; a lot more desert – and then, triumphantly, in the eerie green of night-vision lenses, the explosions of what could only be guided missiles.

For while my plane had crept across the North African continent and I'd consumed plastic cup after plastic cup of G&T in an effort to induce sleep, fighter planes and bombers had been pursuing a somewhat faster route to deliver the first blows of a new – and the second of recent times – offensive against Saddam Hussein's regime.

Arriving at my hotel, I did my best to stop staring at the TV behind the bar – but failed. When I realised the same slime-green night footage was being shown on loop every ten minutes or so, even I became inured to its sinister portents and I toddled off to bed. After a decent night's sleep and a half-decent breakfast, my vim and vigour had returned with added Tabasco.

Dash it if I was going to stay trammelled in my hotel hideaway like a caged beast, I thought; in the best traditions of an Englishman abroad, I would walk among the locals with my head held high, breathing the fresh air of the free man.

And so, after desultory instruction from a bored-looking receptionist, I struck out to explore the best that Sousse had to offer. As I walked, the heat of the morning began to bake the chalk-white pavement, even at this early hour.

I considered what I knew of the situation – which was admittedly little – in a bid to avoid putting myself in potentially awkward situations.

There were still plenty of tourists in town; that much was obvious. There were a fair smattering of Brits, some Germans, a passel of large Americans and a motley assortment of others. But I've never been one to swim with the tide, as it were, and I was determined to get off the beaten track a little and see how Tunisians really lived.

The majority of them are Sunni Muslims; and while I know that the bewhiskered Saddam is a Ba'athist, I can't remember quite how the Sunnis fit into the wider picture. Was I likely to antagonise them with my mere presence? It seems to work with my wife.

However, none of the locals gave me more than a cursory glance as I scuttled deeper towards the old town, dodging scurvy-looking dogs and the kamikaze traffic. And by the time I'd wandered up and down an alley or two of the coolly shaded souk, I was feeling in mid-season form.

Nothing untoward had happened; I was accosted by various hawkers and beggars, but no more than I had braced myself for. And a few of them had even smiled shyly in my direction, instead of reaching for the nearest rock pile and beginning my stoning.

It's fair to say there was a whistle on my lips as I strode down the narrow alleyway bordered by the ancient stone of the town wall. I imagined myself Indiana Jones in search of artefacts; at ease in foreign lands, capable of looking after oneself and making friends with all and sundry. In fact,

I was feeling so full of joi de vivre, that a glass of dark, syrupy coffee and a mid-morning cigar seemed just the ticket. Before I knew it, I'd stepped over the threshold of a nearby doorway and into the gloom beyond.

A lazy ceiling fan beats wobbling circles, wafting hot air around the room; a crooked ginger cat sprawls drunkenly on a table. This is the place for me.

Mr Moustache is, at first, not apparent. I can hear clanking and banging from within, the sound of broom sweeping floor. So, I sit down at a little round table facing the bar, extract my thin cigar and wait with the pleasant and expectant smile of the insouciant traveller.

Pictures on the old television begin to show what appear to be banks of the River Tigris in Baghdad – and an ever-growing crowd of excitable young men who are hell bent on thrashing long sticks about in among the rushes.

Mr Moustache then suddenly pops up from behind the little wooden counter. And our disturbing mime show begins.

He nods, grunts, points, grows hairier by the minute, obviously frustrated, nay incensed, by my imbecilic inability to understand what he's alluding to. I can but grin inanely back, pretend to be absorbed in the contents of my trouser pocket and fleetingly wonder whether I would reach the bright doorway should I choose to make a run for it.

He nods, grunts, points, grows hairier by the minute, obviously frustrated, nay incensed, by my imbecilic inability to understand what he's alluding to.

Getting no response from the imbecilic foreigner opposite him, Moustache leaves his post to clump heavily over. His shadow falls across the table and sweat trickles lazily between my shoulder blades.

I look up.

He bristles, Popeye arms crossed, feline green eyes glaring from under beetling brows that could do with the services of a good thatcher. He waves a brawny arm again and says something in a rumbling, bear-voiced French accent. I now wish I hadn't walked out of my GCSE French exam.

I shake my head apologetically.

Silent images from the screen are showing members of the gathered crowd gingerly peering into the tall grasses, occasionally leaping back as if uncovering a slumbering nest of cobras.

Moustache snorts like a cheesed-off Spanish bull, a noise that sounds like 'TCHA!' – loud and violent in the quiet café. I nod in desperate agreement with him. Tcha! indeed.

Will he pass me over to a gang of extremists, who'll cover my head in a black hood and bundle me into the back of a car? Will I be handcuffed to a radiator and finally grow that luxuriant beard I've often wondered about?

My jelly brain works on the clues I've been given. It's remarkable, the nuances you can pick up from a little guesswork, a jigsaw of footage, a healthy imagination and fear for one's life. I deduce that the TV mob is somehow linked to the alien green night-vision spectaculars that have so far dominated Tunisian TV. That this crowd of reed-thrashers are convinced that a US plane on its way back from such an overnight bombing raid has been brought down and that its ejected pilot, co-pilot – or both – are secreted somewhere along the banks of this ancient Mesopotamian waterway. No doubt the first to find them will get sackfuls of cash, a palace and a lifetime of peer-group envy.

In increasingly frenzied fashion, the crowd on the telly are thrashing their way along the bank and waving their arms around like any self-respecting search party should.

Moustache switches his searing gaze between the TV and me, his upper lip adornment crawling like a poisonous caterpillar. He leans in and blocks my view. And he tries out his English.

'You want?' he rasps in a ruined voice, the ragged fence of teeth revealed again in a wolfish grin. All the better to eat me with.

'No, no, not at all,' I squeak, my heart sliding into canter and my hands scrabbling against the old wood of the chair back.

His beetling brows meet in an infuriated forest thicket and he points, deliberately, again. And it dawns on my tiny, terrified brain, that his finger is pointing not towards the telly now, but back towards the little kitchen behind his counter. From inside, steam is roiling from a bubbling metal kettle, nestled on a charcoal grill.

He points again, looks questioningly. Then he raises a surprisingly dainty hand – little finger out and everything – and proceeds to drink from an imaginary cup.

Tea. It's just tea. He's just asking me if I want a cuppa.

I nearly cry in my broken relief, and vigorous nods and ecstatic hand-shakes ensue. Amid much mopping of my brow and shaking of his leonine head, Moustache departs to prepare another pot of fresh mint tea on his brazier out back. And I'm left with time to breathe and stare into space and convince my heart to stop for a rest. Not literally, you understand; just ease its pace a little.

By the time Moustache has proudly delivered back the stout-coloured, steaming cup – complete with floating toasted pine nuts and a bucket and a half of sugar – I've calmed down enough to insouciantly light the cigar which got me into this fine mess in the first place.

It was ever thus.

✧

Here, I must disagree with Freud. A cigar is *always* more than just a cigar.

This Tunisian tale is one of scores I could give you from my travels over the years where a cigar has led me into – or indeed delivered me from – adventure.

Cigars have introduced me to people that I'd never otherwise have known; taken me places I'd never otherwise have been. I've eaten meals, tasted wines, sampled spirits and had conversations that would have been inconceivable were it not for the involvement of the humble hand-rolled.

This innocent bundle of dried leaves (no chemicals added), lovingly grown, harvested, cured, fermented, rolled and aged, has filled my life with colour, joy and intrigue.

That cigar I smoked, in that Tunisian café all those years ago, was actually the very one responsible for sowing the seeds of this book.

It was a long, thin, elegant Davidoff No.2 – rich and smooth with a wrapper akin to baking parchment dusted with cocoa powder.

I'd pulled it from my travel humidor in Sousse that morning as I planned to wander through the streets of the old town. After Moustache and I had overcome our initial misunderstanding and he had retired to his little kitchen to practise being hairy, I puffed and calmed and watched the blue smoke get chopped into layers by the wobbling fan. I told myself with a relieved chuckle that cigars had got me into plenty of scrapes over the years. And I began to tot them up.

One by one, the list grew; and I began to see a patchwork of people and places, little red flags on a spinning globe that marked each place of travel with an homage to the *puro* – from the Spanish word for 'pure', meaning a cigar made of tobacco from just one country.

It became apparent that much of my adult life – deliberately or not so deliberately, in a variety of intriguing ways – had been defined by the allure of this mystical stick. I investigated further, even ordering a fresh mint tea from my new best friend while I contemplated.

This rich vein of stories spanned a quarter of a century, all my adult life, and connected everything I'd ever done since the age of eighteen. And I've done a fair bit in that time. I've trained as a news reporter; worked as head of copywriting for a blue-chip bank; flown birds of prey for a living; and found peace as a lifestyle and luxury travel writer, meeting new people and seeing new places, from Africa to Asia, through the cigar fields of Nicaragua to the bamboo forests of Japan, from Flanders to the Hebrides and beyond.

> **This rich vein of stories spanned a quarter of a century, all my adult life, and connected everything I'd ever done since the age of eighteen.**

These days I spend a considerable part of my working life writing about cigars too, for magazines across the globe. And I get to combine my love of travel and new people and places with a love for these handcrafted marvels.

I realised that over the years, I had found myself in more than enough cigar-related scrapes to fill a book.

'So why don't you write one then?' I asked myself out loud, risking the furry brow of Moustache wriggling in my direction as I did so.

And why not indeed? I'd learned a lot about cigars and their production by now; had dug out the finest shops in dozens of countries and was on various tasting panels refining my palate to the stage where I could discern and differentiate flavours and nuances that regionally grown tobaccos produce.

My various assignments had given me a vast scope of reference. I'd met and chatted to dozens of the world's best cigar makers and enjoyed their creations in some of the most luxurious and awe-inspiring locations on the planet.

So dammit, I would write the book. And this travelogue was born – a travelogue unlike any you've ever read, I'm sure of that. Whether you like cigars or not shouldn't make a jot of difference to your enjoyment of it, I hope. I write for dozens of magazines and companies about everything from fishing to men's tailoring, great food and wine and artisanal craftsmen and within these pages you'll find tales from my trips and travels which encompass a smorgasbord of epicurean delights.

But if you like the occasional whiff of a well-made smoke, then settle down to enjoy yourself. The cigar finds a place in all the stories that follow. It binds them, much as it does in my memory, as I cast back and remember each one. It's easier for me to remember the specifics of each occasion when I remember the cigar moment that punctuated it; suddenly I can recall the colours, the sounds, the smells. The cigar is a flag in the sand, a moment recorded in time.

Once you're a cigar person you're a member of the gang: a Brother or Sister of the Leaf. You'll have a friend wherever you find a fellow cigar smoker, and what's more, you'll have a friend wherever you find a cigar store or lounge. Wherever you go and whatever you do, there'll be a little cigar-shaped place in your brain that is never fully asleep.

There is a great egalitarian sense of cigar bonhomie – which doesn't exclude ladies, by the way, who are equally welcome – which, until you've experienced it, can't be adequately described.

Cigar people are the *best*.

Once you're a cigar person you're a member of the gang: a Brother or Sister of the Leaf.

Thanks for joining me, Dear Reader, in this sultry alleyway café in Sousse – with sugared mint and the cocoa-like No.2 lingering on our palates. Moustache is clanking away in the kitchen and singing a mournful dirge; the cat still sprawls drunkenly nearby.

I ask you to close your eyes; let the hubbub of the souk and the lugubrious swish of the overhead fan fade from your ears. Like an eddy of cigar smoke, we are shape-shifting, to another time and another destination...

CHAPTER TWO

Bosnia

THE BALKANS PRODUCE MORE HISTORY THAN
THEY CONSUME.

— *Winston Churchill*

I freeze, mid-step, my army surplus boot hovering six inches above the grass. Sunlight reflects off the toecap. It's funny the things you notice.

Beeches sashay at the edge of the glade. Crows lament and wheel above like charred specks of soot; from somewhere nearby comes the *pock pock* of axe on wood.

I shout back over my shoulder.

'WHAT DID YOU SAY?'

In truth, I heard perfectly well the first time, but I want to hear him say it again. I *need* to hear him say it again. My brain can't quite compute what it just heard. I turn my head gingerly to look back.

He's standing, hands on hips, looking like a camouflaged teapot with a blue beret for a lid. Except he's not pouring a nice refreshing cuppa. He's pouring fear – undiluted. It runs down my neck like ice-cold water as he repeats himself.

'*THIS CHAP SAYS YOU'RE IN A MINEFIELD!*'

Then, oh so helpfully: '*DON'T MOVE.*'

I thought that's what he'd said.

In moments like this, time stands still. Just like me.

A few short moments ago this was a gentle stroll in the autumn sunshine. My day had started with a visit to a blown-out Bosnian bridge the Royal Engineers were cheerfully rebuilding. And it was due to finish knee-deep

in snow at the ghostly remains of
a deserted former ski resort, now
deathly still, apart from sluggish
ravens and the shifting wind.

For now, we have stopped our Land
Rover at the top of a picturesque rise,
overlooking a village. Shrouded by leafy hills on either side, smoke gently curling
from stone chimney pots, this slice of rural Bosnia is supposed to be a peaceful
interlude after a morning's somewhat grim tour of the devastation of modern
warfare. We've 'had a brew', as the Army is wont to do every five minutes.

Safely out of the back of the uncomfortable vehicle and with a hot cup
of Rosie Lee inside me, I drift apart from the gaggle of soldiers we've been
hooked up with and thumb the inside pocket of my parka to fish out a little
Montecristo No.4.

It's a ubiquitous Cuban cigar, certainly, a tad *gauche*, perhaps, to those
who know, and love, their smokes. But in these unfamiliar surroundings, the
reassuring *tang* of Montecristo is what I want to ground the recent assault on
my senses.

What I've seen has shocked me to my core.

I fire up the cigar, lighting it reverentially, as always; toasting the end (*foot*
in cigar parlance) first so as not to scorch the wrapper. And then – and only
then – do I gently puff it to life.

My gaze wanders over snaggle-toothed mountains in the far distance, the
snowcaps on their summit having turned from a bruised blue to a warm
blush as the sun soars.

I follow the progress of a jay as it flaps ostentatiously across the clearing,
something large wedged unfeasibly in its bill. And I step away from the road.

I step away from the road.

This is my fundamental error.

From the second I'd landed at Split airport in the rumbling tanker on
wheels that was my Hercules flight from RAF Brize Norton, it had been
drummed into me that Bosnia had been mined to hell and back.

'DO NOT LEAVE THE HARD STANDING!' a cane toad of an officer
had yelled at the motley crew of squaddies and I as we huddled forlornly in a
dank, grey hanger alongside the runway.

'UNLESS. YOU. WANT. TO. DIE!'

To paraphrase his vehement advice, once you're in Bosnia and Herzegovina, you don't go wandering off. If you do, you're likely to become liberally spread over a wide area. I didn't want to explode.

Indiscriminate mine laying during the internal Bosnian war turned large swathes of this once pleasant holiday destination into a deathtrap. Thousands of both soldiers and civilians were killed and maimed over the years (and still are to this day) as an estimated 2.5 per cent of the country's total landmass was littered with deadly landmines. Since the end to hostilities, the best part of 2,000 people have been involved in landmine incidents, more than 500 killed. Many, many more, have had limbs amputated, families destroyed, lives ruined. The clean-up operation continues and is expected, when completed, to have taken twenty years.

It's an evil concept, the landmine – but it ain't new. The Chinese were using versions of them back in the thirteenth century, and ever since they've been used to sow seeds of doubt, fear and destruction among the enemy.

Some simply explode upon accidental detonation. Others contain small pieces of metal, specifically designed to kill, injure or maim as many as possible in a wide arc once deployed. Some jump out of the earth to waist level when activated and spray thousands of deadly fragments in a large diameter. These maiming devices have the added 'advantage' of bringing into the firing line more people in the form of medical personnel coming to the aid of those already injured.

Mines are often left behind as a booby trap for advancing opposing forces. But it's the psychology of mines that interests me. Quite apart from the appalling depravity which must be considered when designing the horrific things (and knowing full well that history shows up to 80 per cent of landmine kills are civilian, a high proportion of these children, with more kills achieved during peace than war), it's the thought process behind setting them before leaving the area – presumably with a dastardly laugh and a twitch of a mutton-greased moustache – which intrigues.

Others contain small pieces of metal, specifically designed to kill, injure or maim as many as possible in a wide arc once deployed.

Landmines are by their nature, indiscriminate in who they kill. This is intended to affect the behaviour of the enemy. But the effect is devastatingly lasting, whether the landmine is activated or not. You get a double bonus with landmines.

For even if they are not activated, *behaviour around them is fundamentally changed*. Decades after they are laid, civilians around landmines are still affected. They have to avoid large swathes of their own countryside. In many cases, hunger and poverty force them to brave these minefields nonetheless, and the stress caused by long periods of not knowing whether each moment is going to be your last, minute after minute, hour after hour, day after day, causes yet more emotional and psychological deterioration. The landmine is truly the gift that keeps on giving.

Each and every landmine also needs a specialist military defuser to dispose of it, because they are designed to detonate if anyone messes with them.

And here I am, right at the beginning of it all. Before a single mission to clear the mines has begun. There are millions of them, everywhere. *And I step away from the road*.

My newspaper has sent me here to shadow local troops on international peacekeeping duties and to find out what it's like to be a Brit serving abroad. Under strict military supervision (and, much to my chagrin, *without* the flak jacket I was secretly hoping I'd get to wear) I've been shown how this once sleepy, largely rural country has been subjected to some of the worst war crimes the mind can imagine.

> # Each and every landmine also needs a specialist military defuser to dispose of it, because they are designed to detonate if anyone messes with them.

Pretty little houses – almost Mediterranean in their appearance – sit cosily alongside each other in thickly wooded hills. The towns are modern, attractive. Tourism was once thriving. But many of these houses now stand blackened, riddled with bullets; streets are smashed, buildings razed. Neighbour has turned on neighbour, lawless militia rule by terror.

In Bihać, as our vehicle bounces along the bomb-scarred road, I take off my cheap woollen gloves and hand them to a snot-nosed child who runs after us. What had he seen? What hardships did he face? Did he and his friends face an uncertain future of dodging landmines and scraping a living?

The trip had been a melancholy, concrete-blackened visit to scenes of depression and savagery – interspersed with getting pissed in the officers' mess. And for several days now, I've managed quite capably to avoid indiscriminately blowing myself up. I've followed the officer's advice to the letter.

I look down and notice the Montecristo is still clasped tightly between my thumb and first finger

Until now.

The thought of the relaxing fragrance of a good, hand-rolled cigar has blown my caution (bad choice of words, perhaps, considering the circs) completely out of the water.

I look down and notice the Montecristo is still clasped tightly between my thumb and first finger; it's pinched in the middle and gasping smoke, which lifts, drifts and eddies away into the greenery.

I consciously release the tension a little in my fingers and bring the dried and rolled bundle of leaves to my mouth for a slow puff. It occurs to me this is the ultimate *Hamlet* moment; I can almost hear 'Air on the G String'.

I release the smoke in a long, shuddering breath and this familiar act – and the reassuring smell of good tobacco – relaxes me. My cocked leg is beginning to ache and jitter and I turn back to my Army friend and his gaggle of colleagues on the road. Surely they're winding me up? This can't really be happening.

My Army sentinel, who has looked after me with gruff kindness for the last few days, is asking urgent questions of a grey, rail-thin chap with a brolly, and the rest of the Land Rover crew are standing about urgently – if one can be said to be standing about urgently. They look worried, anyway.

My guide talks rapidly to the same grey, rail-thin chap who just a few short moments ago was gesticulating and yelling at me in agitation as I wandered from the road. I just thought he'd had one lunch-time *slivovitz* too many. They do that round here. It's a liqueur they make for themselves from plums and they appear to like it. A lot.

I take a deep breath and try to tune into the serenity of my surroundings to ease my racing heartbeat. Now would not be a good time to panic.

When I look down, I notice every nuanced move of my muscles: how my index finger shifts back a quarter of an inch of its own volition when the heat from the cigar end gets too close; how the other fingers curl comfortably behind it in sympathy. I marvel at the fissured pattern of the skin on the back of my hand; the way the tiny hairs can actually feel each sigh of the sirocco breeze across this valley. I'm suddenly – and rather ironically – *uber alive*.

> I take a deep breath and try to tune into the serenity of my surroundings to ease my racing heartbeat. Now would not be a good time to panic.

'OKAY,' shouts my man. I look back.

'HE SAYS THAT THERE COULD BE MINES HERE; NO ONE IN THE VILLAGE WILL WALK ON IT, APPARENTLY. BUT WE THINK YOU'RE FINE. LET'S BE SAFE, ANYWAY. TURN SLOWLY AND WALK BACK CAREFULLY TOWARDS US, AS MUCH AS YOU CAN RETRACING YOUR OWN FOOTSTEPS. OKAY? NICK?'

I look back at him for a long moment, considering my reply. In the end, I can think of nothing pithy, poignant or epitaph-worthy, so I raise a weary hand in affirmation then pivot slowly on one foot – and begin the long walk to freedom. Good name for a book, that.

I gaze down to assess where my previous footsteps are, thankfully, still visible in the wet grass. Then I fix my gaze on the road ahead, the gathered crowd, the Army Land Rover that brought us here, and the anxious faces of my audience, and I take another long breath. As the hairs on the back of pretty much everything stand up, I gingerly re-plant my foot.

Thankfully, there isn't a telltale click from underfoot and I'm not compelled to leap into the air and dismember myself. Mind you, the telltale click is a load of baloney, apparently. Mines are designed to blow you up in double-quick time, not give you a warning so your mates can free you if you're good at playing musical statues.

I take another step. And another. Each one takes a trembling eternity. I can hear the blood singing in my ears. The gang back on the road shouts the

occasional encouraging word as I near; the grey, rail-thin gentleman stands silent, his unfurled brolly limp by his side. The jay returns for an encore, screeching corvid epithets in Bosnian to put me off.

Now I know what a surfer feels like when his mate, safely back onshore, yells that he's spotted a shark. There's an uncontrollable urge to get ashore as fast as humanly possible, back to where your mind and body tell you safety lies. But the laws of physics cannot be shouted down. You still have to go through the motions.

I can't stop my mind racing through these, and other, thoughts. A wave of panic swells and rolls and in turn fires an almost insatiable urge to run, run faster than I've ever done before and I might outrun the dreaded blast. The urge is almost unbearable. I screw my eyes together, shake my head and my military man calls to me, concern obvious in the timbre of his voice.

But instead of running into oblivion, I reach for my cigar. Faithful friend, it clears and focuses my mind, calming those firework neutrons into submission. Doing a *Little-House-On-The-Prairie* style dash across this meadow would not be in my best interests.

> **A wave of panic swells and rolls and in turn fires an almost insatiable urge to run, run faster than I've ever done before and I might outrun the dreaded blast.**

I pause for a moment longer, and – with what I hope appears is a rallying show of nonchalance – take another puff. I move on. The wood chopper is still *pock pocking* in the distance, the callous swine.

Of course, it feels like a lifetime, but within a few short steps, I am back standing on the road amid backslaps and what I choose to interpret as an affectionate bollocking from my Army chums. Their faces say otherwise.

But being British and institutionalised, it's not long before their admonitions gleefully turn to the piss-taking that will continue, relentlessly, for the next five days and nights. When these beloved British soldiers take me to my Hercules ride homewards, they wave goodbye, mimicking arms and legs coming off. What a bunch.

For now, I take a last puff, mentally thank the cigar and toss it into the long grass, where dewfall will extinguish it and decomposition return it from whence it came. I now somehow wish I'd kept it so I could frame it and stick it on my office wall.

Despite the discomfort and unique cold of a two-hour, pothole-marathon of a journey in the back of the semi-open Land Rover, I am asleep in seconds.

And autumn Montecristos will for ever remind me of Bosnia. Poor, ravished Bosnia.

CHAPTER THREE

Leobo

I AM NOT AFRICAN BECAUSE I WAS BORN IN AFRICA, BUT
BECAUSE AFRICA WAS BORN IN ME.

— Kwame Nkrumah

Leobo is like an outpost on Mars.

It stands, proudly isolated, on a great, red pinnacle of rock, sentinel across a vast sweep of scrub and grassland that is this private reserve in the sprawl of the Waterberg mountains.

It's only a pinprick in South Africa on the map, of course. It's impossible to get your head around the vast distances here and how each seemingly huge farm, reserve or estate then disappears into insignificance when you look at a map of the surrounding area.

We are halfway between Gaborone in Botswana and Polokwane in South Africa and already today we've blasted down dirt tracks on quad bikes, scattering pockets of warthog and bemused wildebeest; we've made pizzas by the dam where hippos cough and laugh; somewhat unusually, we've had a tug of war with a crocodile; and had dinner under the piano wire-strung bones of a deceased water horse.

Not one of my more regular days, to be sure.

The creation of an eccentric and adventure-seeking entrepreneur Brit, the Leobo Private Reserve has been put together with a party in mind.

The views are astounding. A vast infinity pool stands overlooking the estate; bedrooms are glass shielded and stare unimpeded across thousands of acres. A research-grade observatory is hidden in the retracting roof in case you fancy a peak at the stars – which frankly, are breathtaking enough by eyeball alone.

I fished in the dam earlier, while one of our guides stood sentinel from the pizza deck above. We'd already met Steve, the regular local croc, and didn't want him putting in an unexpected, grab-your-leg appearance under my rod tip. Steve, you see, has a party piece.

He lurks in the deep, green waters of this dam, which are rich in perch and bass and free from annoying visitors. Except us, of course. He came to the lure, like a well-trained falcon. Except this lure was a frozen chicken tied to the end of a rope.

The six-foot reptile seized the chicken and tried to make off with it. A bizarre game of tug of war ensued, with gloved rangers making sure no one comes off second best in terms of missing arms and legs.

Even the girls – my daughters, who are aged nine and twelve – had a go from a safe distance. And Steve was hauled up onto the beach for my turn where he lay, jade-eyed and hissing, refusing to release his iron clamp on the mangled corpse of the fowl.

By God, he was strong. Even with my mighty strength and the more powerful physique of the guide behind me, he whipped his head from side to side and skittered us closer to the water's edge with ease. He'd no doubt like to see us play the game on his terms and see if we'd still find it fun.

> **A bizarre game of tug of war ensued, with gloved rangers making sure no one comes off second best in terms of missing arms and legs.**

They are something fearsome up close, crocodiles. I watched one once take a zebra as it crossed the Mara River during the migration. Just a calm, log-like drift across the path of the nostril-flaring, wildly paddling zebra and then a paralysing snap of jaws around neck, a swish of murderous tail and a ripple, gently spreading from the spot. Great, monolithic, jagged-backed monsters lay stone dry on the banks, awaiting their turn. We almost always at first mistook them for fallen tree trunks.

Crocs continue to wreak havoc across Africa, as they've done for an age.

Women are targeted disproportionately – not because crocs are misogynists (although one suspects they are – they're *dinosaurs*, after all) but because their favoured method of attack is ambushing those who come down to waterholes or riverways to drink, bath, fish or collect water.

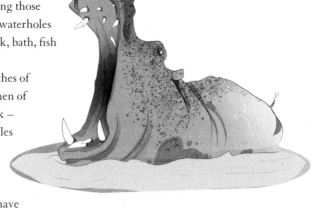

And in huge swathes of Africa, it is the women of the village who walk – sometimes many miles each day – to replenish their water supplies.

Not only do you have to attach a small child to you and keep your hands and head free for carrying loads; not only must you run the gauntlet of dengue fever, malaria, beriberi or cholera; you also have to face the fact that as you bend to fill your container with water, a monster may thrash up from the murky deep and drag you away to an awful death below.

In 2013, matters were made somewhat worse in the Limpopo Province when some 15,000 crocodiles escaped from the Rakwena Crocodile Farm as floods swept through the area.

'There used to be a few crocodiles in the Limpopo River,' said the son-in-law of the croc-farm owner. 'Now there are a lot.'

The Limpopo crocs are perhaps more used to human flesh than we might suspect. Refugees from hunger, persecution and repression in Zimbabwe regularly use the Limpopo River to try to cross illegally into South Africa. Some make it. Others find crocs waiting for them. If you feel like you're in need of some desolation, google 'refugees crossing into South Africa from Zimbabwe'. It's *Heart of Darkness* stuff.

When the river is dry, which it is for many months of the year, the illegal travellers are safe from crocs and hippos. But they are then targeted by the *Guma Guma* – lawless robbers who see the crossing Zimbabweans as little more than a meal ticket – or worse. Young girls get carted off for a life of God knows; men get battered or slaughtered for their meagre possessions.

And when the water flows, these desperate refugees may instead get taken by a huge Limpopo croc. In hindsight, I think I'd prefer the merciless chomp of a saurian than the sordid, drug-fuelled machete of the damned soul of a *Guma Guma*.

Thankfully, our version of the Limpopo Province is somewhat more prosaic. When Steve the croc had finished his party piece and had, with a broad sweep of his own serrated tail, taken the remains of the chicken to the dreadful depths of the dam – and when I'd finished fishing with a decent-sized bass and sunburn, we returned to magical Leobo.

The guides depart and we are left in the tender care of Taryn and Tom, the General and Operations managers at Leobo, respectively – plus our own personal chef, of course. One never likes to travel too far without one of those.

We freshen up with soft spring-fed shower water tingling on our skin. Incidentally, the showers and bedrooms are glass-fronted with sheer, jaw-dropping views across the Waterberg range. It's spectacular, but also a little hard to get used to for a prudish Brit. Soaping one's nether regions virtually al fresco is not something one does that often in deepest, darkest Buckinghamshire.

Refreshed and excited by our other-worldly surroundings, we gather to eat silver service food under the spotlit skeleton of a Waterberg hippo. I have a slight obsession with these great, fat, dangerous, fascinating, fearsome African water horses. This one apparently ran out the loser from a bad-tempered altercation with a white rhino and was painstakingly removed, cleaned and re-assembled on wire overhanging the vast Leobo dining table. This is the sort of madcap project Leobo takes great pride in.

Hippos are another of Africa's most dangerous. A surprising turn of speed for one of such bulk (knew a girl at school like that once, she was unbeatable over the twenty-five-yard dash to the lunch queue) and with a monstrous maw capable of rendering small vessels to matchwood, they are bad-tempered, piggy-sighted and, when congregated in large numbers (or pods as they're correctly called), a bit of a bally nuisance. Apparently, there is one such pod here at Leobo, which, caught in the wrong place, can be quite the adrenaline boost. Our guide told us how a trial of speed between an outraged bull hippo and his quad bike was very much in the balance on one occasion.

The skeletal hippo hanging above our dining table is just another apparition of the style and design here which mixes flawlessly with natural materials and the ochre sand all around. While the surroundings are hedonistic to say the least, with everything the human heart could possibly desire, the atmosphere remains relaxed and joyful. And as mentioned above, there's a frisson of energy about the place – I doubt there's anywhere quite like it in the world.

Jelly the sheepdog wags in to make friends with the girls. We share a glass of intense South African red and a joke with Taryn and Tom, who live further along the escarpment in one of the guest houses, used for overfill when the party really gets started. Their stories of their extraordinary lives here are well worth hearing and with the main house's bar stocked to the gunnels, we're not likely to run out of anything anytime soon. Eventually the pair depart after extracting a promise that we will contact them at any hour should we have the slightest whim.

Fat chance of that – we're Brits abroad and find ourselves being painfully polite and anxious not to put anyone out. Call them up at 3 a.m. because I fancy a spot of night fishing in the dam? Not bloody likely.

But Leobo prides itself on being able to do what others can't, so if there's something you really fancy doing, then by all means ask. Just, for heaven's sake, make sure it's at a sensible hour.

After today – truly one of my most extraordinary ones on God's green earth – we head up to the rooftop terrace and the blue-lit Jacuzzi that steams up there. It's black as a crow's beak outside and cold in the escarpment breeze now. Beyond the halo lights of our castle, Africa rumbles on, shrouded by the dark. An occasional cry or cough from the night echoes up; but it feels like we're the last people left on a very

> **Beyond the halo lights of our castle, Africa rumbles on, shrouded by the dark. An occasional cry or cough from the night echoes up; but it feels like we're the last people left on a very old, very odd planet. We talk to each other intermittently and in whispers in the darkness.**

old, very odd planet. We talk to each other intermittently and in whispers in the darkness.

Then I make the kids laugh by exclaiming at the number of hot tubs there are – actually it's just a reflection of the single tub in the protective surrounding glass. Doh.

We sink into the tub, blood hot, and the wind whips away our voices and the fronds of steam. There's a portable wheelie sound system up here of course, complete with a vast selection of inputs and docks, and I find one which fits my old iPod and search for something appropriate.

And then, weirdly and wonderfully, the cracked pepper tones of Foy Vance spring out into the blackness. He has a history with the Hammonds, although he'll never know it, and now he sings to us and dozens of listening pairs of ears way off in the valley below.

We sink into the tub, blood hot, and the wind whips away our voices and the fronds of steam.

The kids grow silent, tired. And, wrapped in fur blankets, they sit with their mum by lamplight to listen to one more story before bed. There's something Biblical about the three of them in the orange light high up here on the lonely mountain, shrouded with robes, white-faced and cherubic.

I, still in the warm embrace of the Jacuzzi, reach for a cigar. It's an appropriate one for the moment, really; a gift from The King.

The Cohiba Lanceros is an elegant, pencil-thin stick, beautifully made and handed to me with a trademark twinkle in the eye by Edward Sahakian, proprietor of Davidoff London and all-round cigar legend. He is a wonderful man.

His son, Eddie, isn't bad either. Sahakian Junior was helping me compile a few sticks to take away with me one windswept Mayfair morning and while we were pottering in the humidor deciding what would work, Edward couldn't resist getting involved. He offered some quiet words of wisdom, disagreed with Eddie affectionately about a couple of choices, then popped the Lanceros in my top pocket with a nod and a wink and was gone again.

And here – thousands of miles from the yard of soil where it was born, the cigar meets its end. Multilayered with leather and spice, fleeting flavours ghostlike in the darkness, the Cohiba spills forth its message, which is carried away across the Waterberg peaks. Long after the girls slumber, I sit here in darkness and the cigar takes me with it.

CHAPTER FOUR

Youth

AH! HAPPY YEARS! ONCE MORE WHO WOULD NOT BE A BOY!

— Lord Byron

Welcome to the sweet innocence of youth. And the sheer, wonderful stupidity that jogs unwittingly beside it like a faithful dog.

My first cigar arrives unexpectedly in my life when I am an eighteen-year-old idiot on a sunny spring morning. It's a morning overblown with possibility. Birds sing, spirits soar. I positively gambol from bed instead of lolling in it, moaning like a seasick, scurvy sailor. Today is a good day.

My best pal and I have, with the thinly veiled excuse of travelling north to look round a potential university, scored a day off school. Two teenage lads in our own car, skiving school and full of the joys of spring. Can you imagine anything more glorious?

On the way there, we lark and we joke and play rock music at an inappropriate decibel level. Life is good. Along the joyous route we stop to fill up my mate's mum's red Mini Metro. And when we go to pay at the kiosk, the epiphany comes.

Remember that golden glow in the film *Reservoir Dogs* every time the briefcase is opened?

That.

We never get to see what's causing the golden glow in the suitcase of course; I always thought what a nice touch that was from Tarantino. Great bit of storytelling, keeping the audience guessing about what could be so amazing that it stopped people in their tracks in a hypnotic trance.

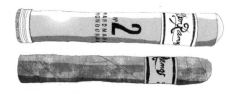

This is me, in the petrol station. My attention, slack jawed though it might be, is entirely caught by a small Perspex box containing five or six metallic tubes within. This wonder is accompanied – in my head at least –– by a chorus of angels and a blinding, shimmering light. I am transfixed by the sight of my first humidor.

I realise now how seafaring men feel as they pass rockbound sultry mermaids offering sly looks and voluptuous curves. I know now why they willingly dive into the waves, never to be seen again.

I turn to my pal with a gormless expression.

'That's what we need,' I say, in hushed, reverential tones.

'What?' he says, turning to the counter with a puzzled expression. 'Condoms?'

'No,' say I, wincing at his crassness in the face of the heavenly. 'Those.'

And I point a shaking finger at the torpedo beauties glimmering shyly at us from beyond their guilded cage.

Of course, in the next few minutes I manage to convince him that spending our lunch money on cigars is the only sane course of action. And he, being also eighteen, daft as a brush, and with the addition of a slightly demented personality inherited from his glorious Sicilian father, is soon convinced this is one of my bestest and brightest. He hands over a crisp tenner and we buy two huge, gleaming tubes.

I wasn't to know at the time – but I know now – that these tubes would change my life.

Back in the car, storming down the motorway, sunroof open and blues being the genre du jour now cranked up to eleven, we open our sealed torpedoes. The cigars inside – I think they were from Don Ramos, a Honduran budget hand-rolled cigar – are mighty truncheons.

I can't recall how we clipped the cap (the small piece of leaf covering the mouth end

I wasn't to know at the time – but I know now – that these tubes would change my life.

or *head* of the cigar). I shudderingly suspect we callously bit them off and spat them out of the window. Forgive me, Dear Reader, for we knew not what we did.

And we light them, as I recall, from the cigarette lighter in the car, nearly torching ourselves in the process, as great clumps of smouldering filler leaf are pulled from the cigar each time we try to move the lighter away from the lit end. I fear we trashed that dear little car as well as the cigars in the course of our next joyous moments.

Tiny pyres are lit around our crotches and on the seats as tufts of billowing tobacco settle there and contentedly puff away. Some of these, like burning debris from a sky-blown fighter plane, blow into the back seat too when caught by the breeze from the open window, and continue their sterling work amid coats, further upholstery, paperwork et al.

We close the windows. And of course, after we've managed to puff alight these great boles of cigars, we puff and billow and fill the vehicle in double-quick time with towering clouds of smoke which threaten to obscure our vision and choke us to death before arrival. I'm surprised no fellow road users call the fire brigade to report a vehicle ablaze.

'Wow!' I splutter, helpfully. It is my first cigar review (some would say one of my best).

We ignore all etiquette and decorum of cigar smoking; we simply don't know it. So, we chew the cigars until the ends became fat wet wedges of goo. We inhale clouds of smoke far more potent than the Silk Cuts we've practised on; we drop ash liberally and without prejudice around ourselves and the vehicle.

Those cigars last all the way up the motorway to Wolverhampton, a journey of nearly one hundred miles. I can recall wondering, thickly, if they would ever end.

We stagger from the little car upon arrival, kippered to the eyeballs and somewhat green around the gills. God knows what the admissions tutor thinks of the two stinking, dishevelled louts who eventually turn up on his doorstep. I guess he's used to it. Suffice to say, neither of us went to his university.

This was my first introduction to the world of *Nicotiana tabacum* – the wondrous plant that the finest cigars are rolled from. It produces beautiful pink flowers (I have one dry-pressed in my office which still reminds me of the day I surreptitiously picked it in the Dominican Republic).

It's a totally different plant than the one used to make cigarettes and other forms of tobacco. And by the way, just to be absolutely clear, cigars are *nothing* like cigarettes.

Imagine a stinking tramp in tattered rags, drooling on a park bench while he slobbers a can of wife-beater, high alcohol, vomit-inducing lager. Now imagine a gentleman of taste and sophistication sitting down to a linen-clad table with a fluted glass of something decanted, aged, exquisitely blended and created. These images, to me, successfully highlight the inherent differences between the lover of the cigarette and the lover of the cigar.

No chemicals are added to cigars to ensure they burn better or last longer. Cigars are lovingly constructed from dried leaves rolled into a tightly packed tube, the skill of the roller allowing just enough passage of air to create the suction necessary to draw smoke through it to taste. That's it.

You won't see cigar lovers huddled under smelly plastic shelters in the rain trying to get their next nic-kick. Neither will they worry themselves silly about long plane journeys; or spending a day or a week without a cigar. I love lobster, but I don't feel inclined to eat one in the rain on a wet Wednesday morning in January because my body is craving sweet lobster flesh. This is fun not a fix.

It's about the flavours, you see, the nuances gleaned from that whirling, swirling smoke so tantalisingly produced by burning carefully grown, cured, aged and rolled leaves. Of course, it's also about the ritual, the Zen-like serenity such an act exudes, the time and permission to relax in a world fraught with clamour and mayhem.

> **Cigars are lovingly constructed from dried leaves rolled into a tightly packed tube, the skill of the roller allowing just enough passage of air to create the suction necessary to draw smoke through it to taste.**

But, when it comes down to it, it's about the smoke. So why the fascination? It's as old as we are. The harnessing of fire – and we all know there's no smoke without fire – was one of mankind's earliest, and still one of its most profound, moments. Families could be warmed, wild animals warned off. Food could be cooked. And it could be preserved by smoke.

Today I have an open fire in my living room, which is watched by the family more than our television, I'm proud to say. We call it Nature's TV. We remain fascinated by fire and smoke: its patterns and vortexes, seemingly random and chaotic shapes and eddies.

People are more honest around an open fire. They are more relaxed around an open fire. Light one on your campsite as the stars come out, for example, and soon you will have a group clustered around, looking into the flames, speaking in hushed tones, revealing themselves, their characters, their thoughts and their fears.

The fascination has remained through millennia. Smoked foods have never been more popular. Artisanal products – smoked salmon, bacon, hot smokes, cold smokes, pre-smoke rubs, glazes and brines.

Smoke imparts flavour in a series of subtle and unique ways. You can burn different woods to give off different odours and flavours. Fruit woods – apple and cherry are favourites – give off a clean and light flavour, while oak is ideal for fish, being delicate and slow burning. Beech is more intense; Americans tend to use sweet and potent woods like mesquite or maple.

Our ancestors began roasting their slabs of woolly mammoth or the delicate rear ham hocks of sabre-toothed tigers a quarter of a million years ago. And yes, hot food with tantalising scorched bits can be a deal more appetising than a slab of soggy, cold flesh. But as well as the flavour of the meat itself – fat rendered and drizzled through the muscle – it's the incredible depth of flavour that smoking wood has imparted that really sets off the taste buds like a Molotov cocktail in a fireworks factory.

Not only did charring your loin of plains' antelope improve its flavour but smoking it gently over aromatic woods also gave it longer life. No longer did Neolithic man have to spend the largest part of his brain wondering how he could find enough warm skins to hide his modesty; now – with a couple of pounds of masticated roast haunch percolating in his belly – he could lie back, pick his teeth with the whiskers of a mastodon and allow his increasingly rich protein diet to fuel his expanding brain. Perhaps, warm and sated after a jolly good nosh, he retires to the old cave (dragging his darling wife by the hair behind him, of course) and indulges in a little soothing cave painting, or writing the rudimentary bars to an early caveman opera.

No, there's no doubt that smoke is a critical turning point in mankind's great journey. And cigar smoke takes this fascination with flavour a step further.

The tobacco grown in a certain spot in a certain field, for example, will harbour certain characteristics unique to that precise plot. In the same way that wine made from grapes from a certain parcel of land may differ significantly in taste profile to another parcel of land – *even if it's just yards apart* – tobacco too, is ultimately the result of its terroir more than anything else.

Minerals in the soil impart subtle flavours in the tobacco; it's been suggested that other crops perhaps previously grown in the soil may also find their way into the leaves and ultimately the smoke and the taste. I haven't discussed this theory in any depth with any tobacco farmers or manufacturers, but coffee and cocoa are often rotational crops in soil where tobacco is regularly grown. Coffee and cocoa also happen to be two of the more commonly prevalent flavours found in cigar smoke, so who knows – maybe there's something in it. Having said that, leather is a common base flavour too and, as far as I know, they don't plant old motorbike jackets in fallow years.

It is the balance and nuance of these flavours which shift and change throughout the 'life' of a good hand-rolled cigar. These delight and intrigue cigar lovers and also change with time, giving the very best cigars an allure like that of vintage wine, to be laid down and drunk (smoked) at various intervals over the years.

For the sake of clarity, cigar smokers don't inhale – inhaling is purely a way of obtaining maximum nicotine absorption into the bloodstream. Cigar smokers *taste*.

No, there's no doubt that smoke is a critical turning point in mankind's great journey. And cigar smoke takes this fascination with flavour a step further.

They taste the artistry of the cigar blender and roller. Each cigar features whole leaves and sometimes parts of whole leaves, to achieve a desired and very specific blend and taste. Leaves from different parts of the tobacco plant have different characteristics. The ones nearer the top and therefore the sun tend to be thicker, more full-flavoured. Those nearer the base of the plant have less taste and flavour, yet a far better combustibility when dried, fermented and burned.

This subtle jigsaw puzzle of natural products, more art than science, is what we love about cigars. It's exactly the same principle as growing and making great wine or batches of phenomenal coffee.

Each hand-rolled cigar may pass through 200 pairs of hands before it reaches the smoker. Hundreds of procedures need to be done correctly to make sure the cigar reaches you in perfect condition. It's not hammered out of a factory machine at a rate of millions a day.

All of which may help you to see why cigar lovers are dismayed when they are lumped in with cigarettes – junkies in the eyes of the anti-smoking zealots – and of the law.

Every time a new measure is imposed to wean people off cigarettes, the peace-loving cigar man is punished. Each time an excruciating new label is attached – or a prescription for plain packaging pronounced – the cigar lover, who simply wants to enjoy the occasional artisanal masterpiece with like-minded individuals, is targeted.

Kids don't wander around smoking cigars. They don't pass the window of a tobacconist, take a glance in and think to themselves, 'Ooh, I could murder a Cohiba.'

Cigar smoking is a legal, adult, lifestyle choice; just as drinking alcohol is.

I am determined this shall be a book of joy, a celebration of the cigar, with no room to sully its pages with the shouters, the brayers, the self-righteous and the small-minded. I'm here to tell you that cigar people are great people. Those that make these works of art, and even most of those who enjoy them, are the sort of folk who embrace the light and banish the dark. And the dark side has no place in this story.

Although, now I come to mention it…

CHAPTER FIVE

Star Wars

WHAT WE WANT IS A STORY THAT STARTS WITH AN
EARTHQUAKE AND WORKS ITS WAY UP TO A CLIMAX.

— *Samuel Goldwyn*

It's not every day you fire up a fat stogie on Tatooine.

My first extra-terrestrial smoke – sort of – came amid the formidable dunes of Tunisia on the site of one of film's most famous landscapes.

You may or may not know that the country has long been a destination for the die-hard *Star Wars* fan. Scenes from no less than the first six movies (whichever order they are currently configured in; they lost me with the Roman numeral shenanigans right from the get-go) were shot in various parts of this ancient and intriguing country.

The canyon where Luke Skywalker first comes across Obi-Wan Kenobi? Right here. The vast dunes where C-3PO and R2-D2 crash-land and wander off to meet Jabba the Hutt? Amid Tunisian desert. And the legendary Skywalker farming ranch that Luke so pines to leave? Here in the old town of Matmata.

Not to be confused with the 'new' Matmata, this famously recognisable place is the site of the extraordinary Tunisian troglodytes. It's an evocative, if unfortunate, name for simple underground-dwelling folk. To me, it conjures up images of trolls gnawing on the bleaching bones of small children, but I'm sure they don't do such a thing. Often.

They're ordinary people trying to get on with their lives. Only they live underground. And look like walnuts.

Well, the one I saw looked like a walnut. She was about 200 years old, wizened like a sun-ripened raisin, her deeply fissured face beaming with

anticipation of foreign dinars as my busload of intrepid explorers approached her village, preceded by the oily charm of our Berber guide.

It is searingly, soul-searchingly, eye-ball-dryingly hot. Every surface smoulders. Nothing lives above ground. Human – indeed any – habitation seems a remote possibility.

Our guide explained to us, back in the glorious, forehead-caressingly cool air conditioning of our coach, that this little settlement was where the original Skywalker Ranch was filmed in the 'first' *Star Wars* movie. Of course, the coach was packed with *Star Wars* geeks that already knew this. Why else would they be traipsing across the desert to meet some walnuts? And then there is me. Always the thirst for knowledge. Nothing to do with *Star Wars*. What. So. Ever.

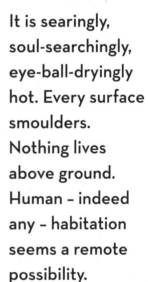

It is searingly, soul-searchingly, eye-ball-dryingly hot. Every surface smoulders. Nothing lives above ground. Human – indeed any – habitation seems a remote possibility.

On the road to Matmata, the bleak, featureless horizon stretches into the endless desert. Yet suddenly we are upon them. The troglodytes have dug into the scorched earth to build a life here. Turns out they were absolutely right to do so.

Despite the ground temperature being roughly equivalent to the surface of the sun or a freshly toasted pop tart, the change in temperature from the surface to the chamber entrances just a few feet below is remarkable. The whitewashed walls, sleeping scraggy dogs and little pots of flowers are suddenly more Mediterranean than subterranean.

It's still warm of course, but it's bearably warm. We descend cautiously, perspiringly, to the main courtyard where the Skywalker ranch is instantly recognisable. A strange feeling, this familiarity, in a world so utterly alien.

We gawp and smile and look around us in wonder. How clever the location chappies were back in the late seventies.

And then I see her – the walnut. Miss Matmata 1903 smiles at me through ragged tombstones of teeth, worn by time (and the bones of small children, obvs). She sits on the floor in a patch of shade, her spindly, sun-darkened legs crossed easily and some knickknack in her lap, undoubtedly for sale to passing foreign mugs with too much money.

Her face has the contour lines of an aerial-mapped, mid-drought delta; deep canyons and tributaries spreading like blood vessels, disappearing into the mountainous landscape of nose and eyes.

I'm doing this fine lady a disservice of course, for she welcomes us warmly into her home and grins gappily as our guide gives us the lowdown on the area, its history and its people.

She reminds me of Gagool, the crone in Rider Haggard's fabulous *King Solomon's Mines*, which I read over and over again as a bloodthirsty boy. I smile back at her and wonder if she'd appreciate my advice: don't scramble under descending stone doors anytime soon.

Our guide drones on and on and despite the stultifying heat above, I'm just about able to keep track of what he's saying. Apparently, it wasn't until the late 1960s that the world at large became aware the troglodytes were living in Tunisia. I guess you wouldn't know they were there unless you inadvertently stuck a foot down a troglodyte hole while its inhabitant was coming up for air. So, they got on with their lot and everybody else pretty much left them alone.

One year, heavy rains flooded these underground homes and tunnels and literally flushed the entire population out. The authorities were contacted and a civil servant came out, stared goggle-eyed at the little caves under the scorched earth, gave a low whistle and then got on to the builders to knock up what is now modern-day Matmata.

Or something roughly along those lines occurred. Please excuse my abridging, but I've got an air-conditioned coach to catch.

A new smart town was constructed with actual street level housing. But the ungrateful old trogs didn't want to live in smart high rises (and I raise my non-existent hat to 'em because of it).

Most of them moved back to their burrows – sorry, homes – once they'd dried out. And these days, irreverent arses like me come along and gawp at them for a few minutes before leaving some crumpled dinar notes and zooming off to see the Roman Amphitheatre at El Djem.

Such is a troglodyte's lot.

As mildly chuffed as I am to recognise the little entrance where Uncle Owen, Aunt Beru and Luke shared a petulant meal, I'm getting a bit fed up with the over-zealous idolatry being practised by some of our party (notably some voluble Americans, I'm duty bound to tell you).

They seem to never tire of having their pictures repeatedly taken in front of non-descript walls while striking middle-aged Jedi poses and making swishing noises with imaginary lightsabres. This is most definitely not what I signed up for when I came to Tunisia to learn about its culture, history and heritage. Well, why did you sign yourself up for the trip to a *Star Wars* filming location then? I hear you ask. And I would reply, pompously, that it was indeed for the coliseum at Ej Djem and then I'd cough self-consciously and stalk away, hands stiffly clasped behind my back, to studiously inspect a brick on a nearby wall.

But as you're not here at this time, instead I reach into my backpack for the faithful screwtop tube I have ensconced within. It's time to take a chill pill – in the form of a Scooby Snack of a cigar.

The Le Hoyo Du Maire from Hoyo De Monterrey (Cuba) has stood the test of time. It's always well made, light in strength and has a sweet spot that tantalises the palate like a butterfly tiptoeing across a thistle head.

I'd happily give one to a first-time smoker – and gratefully receive one myself anytime, they're that good. Incidentally, they've since been discontinued by Habanos SA, the Cuban government-owned company responsible for the growing, manufacture and distribution of the country's cigars worldwide. Cue much gnashing of teeth. But if you know the right people and are willing to wear out a bit of shoe leather, you can still find wonderful aged boxes of these small elegant smokes and I urge you to do so.

I fish out my trusty inexpensive cutter and an equally cheap torch lighter (I rarely travel with high-end cigar kit – it just gets nicked, lost or battered beyond repair). And I make my quiet excuses to step up topside for a few sacred moments of peace away from Luke Skywalker wannabes. I feel like I need to be alone and to soak up a little of this strangeness in my own, silent manner.

Big mistake, young Padawan.

I poke my head above the parapet and a furnace blast of heat seals my chops like a flame-grilled whopper. I reckon I can easily light my cigar on the flaming sand crystals around me, it's that hot. I consider disappearing back downstairs and submitting to handing Miss Walnut fistfuls of moolah before we can get out of here.

But just then a particularly loud lightsabre swoosh reaches my ears and I scramble from the hole like…well, like a flood-flushed troglodyte.

Shielding my tender, pasty Brit skin, I look overhead to where the sun boils like a nuclear-treated egg yolk. Now if you've ever had a hankering for a cigar, you'll know that it takes a lot to put you off, wherever you may be. An awful lot.

It's not that you're a wheezing, choking, Gollum-like addict, as I've already explained. But sometimes the time is right for a cigar; mine often act as punctuation to a lot of my memories and experiences. I often remember a particular time, place, even emotion by conjuring up which cigar I was smoking at the time, so if the opportunity slips by, often so does the mental underlining that might have taken place.

I often remember a particular time, place, even emotion by conjuring up which cigar I was smoking at the time, so if the opportunity slips by, often so does the mental underlining that might have taken place.

I therefore hate to give up on a cigar, if I can at all avoid it. Hurricanes in the Hebrides, monsoons in the jungle – I've always managed to find time and space to fire one up and add another punctuation mark to the chapters of my existence. And of course, I'm a stubborn sod too, which helps. My resilience is legendary.

Once I wandered the entire outdoor circumference of a Scottish castle and examined every nook and cranny in search of a tranquil spot. This despite the fact that the wind was roaring in from the seas and the rain was lashing down at right angles. I found my spot though – there nearly always is one, if you look hard enough. It was tucked in between two crenellations, which gave a small relief to the living room windows.

By that time of night, it was dark and quiet and everyone sensible inside was tucked up in bed. Not I. I'd helped myself to a last snifter from the generous laird's malt Scotch collection and begun my search. There, in a pocket of calm roughly three feet wide, I torched a little cigar from Rafael Nodal's Aging Room stable. And I stood, listening to the lash of the rain and the sodden wind and the roar and clash of red stags all around me. Magical.

Anyway, I digress. Suffice to say that a little sunshine wasn't going to spoil my chance to mentally mark Matmata. Instead of admitting defeat and scampering back down, mole-like, to the cooling quarters of the walnuts, I tightened my grip on my lighter and singed the cigar.

If Yoda was here – and let's face it, it's not impossible, given the circs – he would be shaking his little fuzzy head and perhaps mumbling something like 'Idiot, he is.' Mad dogs and Englishmen and all that.

But Yoda's not here that I can see and I am able to walk a short distance away from the noise and sprawl of the troglodytes' home and admire the panorama of the desert. The Sahara runs through Tunisia as it does much of North Africa. I have a little pot of its timeless, ceaseless, incredibly fine sand trapped in a box frame in my house.

And although it's a stark and at times sinister place, it's also incredibly beautiful. I manfully ignore the blazing sun and sear the moment into my memory.

If truth be told, this just isn't the finest place to savour the more refined aspects of tobacco grown in the hallowed Vuelta Abajo – Cuba's answer to the Loire Valley. In fact, this place is only really suitable for savouring tobacco grown in Death Valley. Of which there is precisely none, of course, it being one of the hottest places on earth, with a rather warming 134-degree-Celsius world-record air temperature supposedly achieved in the early twentieth century.

So, the chefs among you may nod knowingly when I begin to talk of that stage of cooking when a well-larded joint of pork begins to transmogrify into juicy crackling. There is an intermediate stage of sticky rubberiness which it must go through in order to achieve that perfect hard-to-the-tap finish we so desire.

Picture me then, as I stumble back down into the seeming Stygian darkness of the troglodyte home after just twenty minutes or so toasting under the old Tunisian sunbed. My skin is going through the aforementioned crackling process. And it's turning a deepening shade of vermillion by the second.

One moment I thought I was fine, the next I could feel the world slipping away.

My eyeballs are bulging from my pounding head and my swollen tongue flops sullenly inside my mouth like a beleaguered beluga. I cling to the wall for support and croak for water. It feels like I've swallowed a haggis whole, and its dorsal fin is stuck in my larynx.

The crowd, still patiently queuing to be fleeced by old mother walnut, turns and gasps in horror at this apparition which has stumbled from the desert above. Never mind *Star Wars*; picture scenes from *The Mummy* and you won't be far away.

Our guide rushes over with a worried look upon his face while I melt into a puddle on the cooling courtyard floor. He pours cold water down my throat and on my head. I don't know it now, but I've gone a long way to ruining the rest of my Tunisian adventure by being a stubborn old cigar smoker. Hey, who hasn't suffered from a dose of good old-fashioned, self-induced sunstroke anyway?

Wiping salty sweat from a delirious eye, I notice Gagool is looking fixedly in my direction with a knowing wink and a toothless smile.

Ooh, she's a fine looking woman, that one. It's a troglodyte's life for me.

CHAPTER SIX

Cuba

GRACE WAS IN ALL HER STEPS, HEAVEN IN HER EYE, IN EVERY
GESTURE, DIGNITY AND LOVE.

— *Milton*

Incidentally, the fairer sex are very often the finest cigar rollers you can find.

I'm not sure if this is because they are more patient, have a gentler touch or are just clever enough to realise what a good job a high-class roller can enjoy, but it is the case that in many of the cigar factories I've had the pleasure of visiting, lady rollers often far outnumber the men.

As is the case in Cuba's remarkable El Laguito factory, where Cohibas are created behind a curtain of secrecy. Cohiba may be brand name known to you even if you're an ingénue in the world of fine, hand-rolled cigars. It is an absolute mark of luxury. Its smart gold, black and white livery is renowned the world over.

Cohiba was originally brought into being by none other than Fidel Castro, would you believe. Back at the height of his popularity and power after his successful revolution, he was a big smoker of cigars. After all, it was what Cuba was famous for. Both he and Che Guevara were fond of *lancero*-sized cigars, elegant, pencil thin, long smokes which can only be made by the most skilful rollers at the factory.

He was walking with one of his bodyguards one day and noticed he had a cigar in his top pocket. Being *El Jeffe*, he helped himself and loved the resultant blend. He asked the bodyguard where he got the smokes, found the roller – and employed him purely to make cigars for him from then on.

From these inauspicious beginnings, the rich, creamy, luxurious style of Cohiba was founded. At first, these smokes were occasionally handed out as official Cuban diplomatic gifts. Eventually, they became their own line using only the best Cuban tobacco and promising to be the best the island had to offer.

It's not open to the public, El Laguito, but if you are well known or have some suitably eminent friends, then it's possible to obtain an unofficial tour of this one magnificent townhouse in a posh suburb of Havana.

When I first went to Cuba, I wasn't particularly well known; but I was with the eminent Mitchell Orchant of C.Gars Ltd – whose shops the length and breadth of the UK have breathed new life into what was fast looking like a moribund cigar business.

From his own front room, he has built a cigar masterpiece – a Death Star, if we're to over-egg the *Star Wars* metaphor – and has long been the supplier of a good story, a gracious host and, most importantly, a friend.

And so, I only need to wave Mr Orchant's face in the general direction of the El Laguito security, and we are inside. It's good to be The King.

If you've never had the opportunity to smoke a cigar in a cigar factory – I can only commiserate. It is akin to sampling an oyster you've just loaded onto the boat at Colchester; tasting the smoked salmon you caught on the Tweed yesterday; sipping a single malt beside one of the

mighty Speyside washbacks; dipping your lobster into the butter sauce in New England.

Let me give you a flavour of what it's like to walk into a Havana cigar factory.

El Laguito is in a cultured backwater of Havana. No dilapidated buildings here. Grand colonial dwellings with wide expanses of lawn flash past as your cab brings you closer and then you're there, in front of a cream and gold sizeable 'home' set well back from the road. There is little to outwardly suggest that you are calling on perhaps the world's most prestigious cigar brand, or *marque*.

The heat and light from outside are cranked up to eleven and when you step indoors – although there's no air con and the air is merely pushed around a bit by a few ceiling fans – it feels a relief.

This old house will be interesting and stimulating enough if you're not a cigar lover. But if you are, expect a rise in pulse rate. The smell of ageing *pilónes* of tobacco, overlaid with the faint tang of the ammonia being given off by the fermentation process; the sound of a hundred voices, talking Spanish at a million miles per hour; the unmistakable tang of a freshly rolled Cuban cigar. The sunlight streams through high windows and pinpoints the burnished gold of Cohiba colour that lines the wall of the grand sweeping staircase before you.

You can wander among the maze of crumbling rooms, which are mostly staffed with ladies, as previously mentioned, and consider how the very finest craftsmen (and women) make working with their tools look ridiculously easy.

Have you ever had the pleasure of watching one of the ladies of Cromer handpicking the town's famous crabs, for instance? It's extraordinary. The speed and dexterity of their nimble fingers darting across the jagged shells has to be seen to be believed, although the romantic image of aproned matriarchs working from some beach hut with sand in their hair was somewhat ruined by my visit to a purpose-built Cromer factory where they wore wellies and Smurf-like blue headgear.

The point is that the effortless way they worked their way methodically around the freshly boiled carapace of crab made it look like any fool could do it. And this fool had a go and speared himself with the picker.

The ladies of El Laguito also demonstrate a casual ease as they work tobacco.

The cigars they handle, cajole, caress and create are as extensions of their extravagant fingernails. (One would have thought long fingernails would have been a definite no-no with the large amount of expensive wrapper tobacco they work with, but hey, this is Cuba.)

The smooth, million-times-practised blur of their hands is mesmeric as they shuttle from tobacco bundle to *chaveta* – the purpose-made guillotine knife they use to cut the leaves.

In just a couple of minutes, another beautifully formed cigar is born and stacked neatly with his brothers and sisters, ready for further dressing in bands and boxes elsewhere in the factory.

The cigars they handle, cajole, caress and create are as extensions of their extravagant fingernails.

There will be someone official hovering near you at El Laguito – that's just the way it is in Cuba. You can't go wandering off piste. They don't like it. So while access is pretty free, you're still not quite at your leisure. If you try and retrace your steps to enter a room you haven't been shown into – you may find a firm pressure on your elbow as you're led away. Get used to it. This is Cuba.

The smell in the factory is magnificent. Deep, chocolate-smooth wafts of very, very good tobacco leaf. It's a smell that quickens your pulse and makes your heart leap with joy. At least it does mine. If you're a connoisseur, a visit to a cigar factory is an uplifting, almost spiritual experience.

Except, perhaps, for the fermenting room. Here, leaves are hung like thirsty bats in the humid atmosphere and misted with water. The heat and humidity do their work, drawing out the impurities from the leaf, and in particular the smelling salt choke of ammonia, which fills the air. It is truly stultifying. Only the foolish or the hardy can stand it for more

The smell in the factory is magnificent. Deep, chocolate-smooth wafts of very, very good tobacco leaf. It's a smell that quickens your pulse and makes your heart leap with joy.

than a few seconds. The eyes weep, the nostrils flare and you flap your way out again, trying to breathe. Just like being caught in the perfume counter at Selfridges, really.

During my tour of El Laguito, we were given unbanded Behike 56s to smoke; they'd not long been released onto the market. You, I'm afraid, won't be so lucky. Not because I'm anything special, but because you can't find Behike 56s these days for love nor money. At the time of writing, Cohibas of all sizes, but particularly the outrageously popular Behike line, haven't been rolled in any great numbers for many months. There just isn't enough tobacco of the size and quality needed, so production has been halted. I personally find this rather gratifying, in a perverse kind of way. (I might feel differently if I was a regular BHK smoker, but being lacking in sufficient quantities of the folding stuff, I'm not.)

At least Habanos SA are not trying to fob us off with lesser tobacco labelled up as Cohiba. The beauty of a natural product is, surely, that it is *real*; it changes with the seasons, changes when you expose it to different conditions and is precious because, in a way, it is limited. Isn't that why we love asparagus, or grouse, or English strawberries?

If there's been a poor crop or a natural disaster, which ultimately means less or even no tobacco of the necessary grade can be grown, then I am content to wait until it can. And I'll look forward to it all the more because of it.

As I was saying, the BHK 56: a great fat powerful stick, laden with *medio tiempo* – the rare and little-used 'extra' leaf that sometimes grows on the upper parts of the tobacco plant. It creates an utterly unique taste on the palate – I once opined that it offered a swipe of taste like a butter knife across the palate. It remains one of the more sensible things I've ever said.

A word of warning here. Smoking cigars in Cuba is not like smoking them anywhere else. First, you'll find they keep going out, because more often than not, they're over-humidified. You just can't keep them dry enough when you're out and about as the island is so damned humid.

And second, before any visit to this Mecca of hand-rolled delights, you might need to go into training beforehand. This isn't a small panatela, post-dinner kind of existence. This is serious cigar stuff and you will want to make the most of your time here. If you're with a hardcore cigar crowd, you'll likely fire up your first shortly after finishing your coffee and eggs in the morning – and lay down your last just a few hours shy of breakfast the following day. Sounds grim to the uninitiated, but in Cuba, having a stogie in your mouth feels *right*. Like drinking a daiquiri next to Hemingway's statue at El Floridita. Or being offered fake cigars on the street (never buy them. They're fake).

An existence for the faint-hearted, it ain't, that's for sure, so you'll need plenty of water and rest before you go – you won't get much sleep when you're there, believe me.

Following my El Laguito experience, I take a day trip to the famed Pinar del Río region, home to the world's finest cigar tobacco.

It's a long, pot-holed, dusty, warm drive to get there, mind. And as we speed past donkeys, scabby dogs, pick-up trucks laden with unspeakable amounts of logs, bales, boxes and/or people, I take the opportunity to fire up another Hoyo de Monterrey – this time an Epicure No.2.

If you're with a hardcore cigar crowd, you'll likely fire up your first shortly after finishing your coffee and eggs in the morning - and lay down your last just a few hours shy of breakfast the following day.

If you were to maroon me on a desert island and give me one last current production stick to last, I'd pick this one. It never disappoints and it offers something different every time you light one. Yes, it's mild; no, it's not overly complex. But it is rich, smooth, delicate and balanced; sweet and refined and never lets you down.

And so I sit, with the window down, smoke escaping from my lips like the thoughts drifting through my brain; and I watch Cuba go by.

The countryside looks prehistoric. Great, vine-covered outcrops rear from the earth; shaggy, overgrown mountains loom; and the rich, rust-red soil is everywhere toiled over. Scimitar-horned oxen toss their heads and stumble through it, urged on by a farmer, stripped to the waist and gleaming with sweat. Only a threadbare straw hat keeps the merciless sun away.

Small clusters of villages – often no more than a ramshackle collection of tin huts, scrawny chickens and the occasional gaudy sign for a bar – spring up and fade into the distance as you go.

And as you get into the Vuelta Abajo proper, you are followed by vultures. Turkey buzzards tilt on upturned wing above the ever-encroaching greenery. I get the impression that if you turn your back for an instant in Cuba, something grows.

Creepers dangle from improbable limestone outcrops. Deep, dank, dripping crevices lurk, where alligators slumber through the heat of the day. Anything that isn't shaded bakes.

Here among the plantations, tobacco seeds are cultivated carefully indoors, separated as seedlings and sown out when sturdy enough. In around fifty days, they will stand seven feet tall and have vast umbrella-like leaves of varying thickness, depending on their position on the plant and exposure to the sun.

And the great game of variables begins. As in wine, a multitude of factors will determine the quality of the finished product.

Where was it grown? Details such as the very acre of soil will make a difference to taste. Was it sungrown or, more commonly, grown under shade? How was rainfall that year? At what stage were the leaves harvested? Were they safely cured in open-air barns?

These and a hundred other considerations are pondered by the Cuban tobacco farmer. And that's before the leaves are bundled and brought into the factory for sorting, ageing and eventually, rolling. Growing and making cigars is truly an act of devotion.

After another long, bumpy jaunt back to Havana, we summon up enough courage – and enough cigars – to catch the late show at The Tropicana. This famous old club was the playground of the rich, famous, shady

and downright dangerous back in the day. Sinatra, Brando, Wayne and Hemingway; Marciano, Marilyn and Mafiosi. A hedonistic gathering of the glitterati have cavorted in Cuba and nowhere is this better typified than at this carnival cage of a cabaret.

Remember the opening scene in *Goodfellas*, where Ray Liotta's Henry makes his way through the bowels of a club to the feet of the stage to be greeted warmly by the headline act?

That's how this place makes you feel.

Broads and dudes swarm by the entrance as you climb from your Cadillac. Tuxedoed attendants dash to welcome you in the warm night air, the muggy breeze soughing through the spotlit palm trees. You pull a roll of notes from your pocket, peel off a generous wedge and crumple them into the outstretched palm of your grateful driver. Then, you disappear into the twilight inside.

It's a curious mixture of indoor and out; open air and nightclub; opulence and negligence. Night-attired beauties flit. You grab a tumbler of rum from a passing tray and mingle.

Soon, you're compelled to push your way through the throng to the auditorium. It's like a giant pterodactyl enclosure, arched and glassed, with the swaying fronds and stars visible outside. Within, it's hot and noisy and an almost tangible sexual frisson of electricity bounces from crowded table to crowded table.

A waiter, almost on the run, unceremoniously dumps a bottle of Havana Club rum and a bucket of ice on the table. And you pour yourself a generous slug and torch another Cohiba Behike.

> It's a curious mixture of indoor and out; open air and nightclub; opulence and negligence. Night-attired beauties flit. You grab a tumbler of rum from a passing tray and mingle.

Tonight, it's a Behike 52; squat and bulbous, like a fat-lipped Edward G. Robinson. You chew it wetly, savouring that telltale butter knife swipe of *medio tiempo* across your palate.

You drop a single ice cube into your tumbler. The lights dim to a hiss of expectation and suddenly, with a rolling boom akin to thunder and a squeal of horns, this party gets started.

Scores of gorgeous dancing girls clad in feathers strut, bump and grind their way around the multilevel stage. Lights pulse in time to the seedy, sensual, irresistible Cuban rhythm. It's voodoo, hypnotic. Your jaw is slack, your mouth dry. Another swig of rum. You've never seen a show like this.

Seemingly without pause, this cabaret to end all cabarets rolls from skit to skit: dancing, singing, acting and acrobatics, underlaid by a red-hot live band that barely draws breath.

There's only time for open-mouthed stares at fellow-goers – it's too loud for any meaningful conversation. Lightning flashes from the stage intermittently reveal the ghostly auditorium, packed with tables like yours, glued to the stage.

You'll find that bottle of rum on the table won't last long; you'll be thirsty tonight like never before. You raise your hand and eventually an eagle-eyed waiter sees it and brings another. You may also find that Behike the best cigar in living memory, for there's no greater place to smoke it.

Imperceptibly, the minutes stretch on and the action never lets up. Dozens of costume changes are racked up; sets change, pace quickens and slows. And by the denouement of this extraordinary two-hour spectacle, the place is a steamy, boozy bear pit, enraptured by the performance.

The final scene is a campy caveman sketch with a barely covered blonde bombshell vying to escape from marauding hunters. She runs this way and thither, climbing the scaffolding of the stage until she is 'treed' and unable to escape.

Tension mounts and the drums pound out a primal beat. And then, defiantly she steps out and swan dives into thin air. There's a collective gasp of horror from the audience before she is caught by the bevy of cavemen below and triumphantly carried aloft from the stage.

It's a staggering moment of bravado and the audience breaks out into a standing ovation. You stand, barely breathing, the stub of a mangled cigar clutched in one paw and the dregs of yet another rum in another.

Tropicana is a show you'll remember all your life.

Litter ripples amid the backwash in the bay and on the gentle waves, under a sweltering sky, a man paddles in slow motion in his homemade boat.

This boat – maybe five feet by three – is made entirely of polystyrene foam blocks lashed together. The oar is an offcut of wood, laboriously worked into a paddle shape by hand. Through my binoculars, I can also see on the prow

of his proud vessel a pair of homemade flippers, once again shaped into long flat paddles to help him descend to the seabed – and rise from it – as fast as possible. He has no scuba gear of course, so he needs to get down to the shellfish as soon as he can.

Mask and snorkel are the only things he hasn't been able to fashion for himself and I wonder just how he got his hands on these relatively expensive luxury items. Like everything else in Cuba, there'll be a story behind it.

Nothing is quite as it seems here. Sure, at first glance, Havana looks a lot like the sort of sunshine city haven we all wish we could live in. Racial and religious harmony, lots of free time, an attitude that can only be described as 'live and let live' and a social life most of us can only dream of. But then again, we don't have to be careful which opinions we express in public. We're allowed, within reason, to travel freely and without question, to go wherever we like in the globe. We can launch and own businesses with minimal government interference. The same can't be said of Cuba.

The amateur fisherman is stripped to the waist, burned teak by the sun, and he's taut with muscle. You don't see many fat folk over here: rationing remains in place. When he dives from his boat, he keeps another foam block floating above him as a marker of his progress. Before continuing my study from a distance, I retreat under the awning of the seaside villa I'm staying in. It's not yet mid-morning in November – but it's blisteringly hot.

When he eventually returns to the boat, he's hauling a netful of shellfish. Scallops? I can't tell. He clambers aboard, shakes seawater from his black locks in a rainbow spray of colour and sets off paddling to the other side of the bay.

I must admit that in the heat my head is thumping. It's Day Four in Havana and it's fair to say the metaphorical foundations are starting to crumble. As you may already have gathered, this is no city for a cup of cocoa, an improving book and an early night. It's a place to party. Every night of the week.

Last night, for instance, was memorable. Stopping for dinner and a few cold glasses of beer, the crowd I was with moved on leisurely from bar to bar. If you think Havana is romantic during the day, you should see it at night. It's almost Gothic: lights, where they are available, splash across the tumbling skyscape of apartment blocks and church spires. Dark alleys, shadowy doorways and inviting arches both warn and entice.

Nothing gets going early here, so bar hopping is the order of the day. Everyone seems to know everyone else and music thumps out of every bar.

It's impossible not to get dragged into the atmosphere, even if you try. You may be reluctant for another night on the town, seeking nothing more than a good night's sleep to reset the balance. But you're not likely to get it.

Once you're out, you're caught in the net.

At some time in the early hours, I was *introduced to* El Gato Tuerto – the One-eyed Cat. It's in the Vedado neighbourhood, directly under the infinitely cool shadow of the Hotel Nacional.

To one side is the mighty Malecón – the iconic sea wall that stretches along the capital's Pacific seafront for over five miles. It's a nocturnal meeting spot for Cubans. They sit on the wall, play music, drink, rum, fish, make love and Lord knows what else, as the salty spray lashes the air around them. It's intoxicating. Or at least it would be if one wasn't already intoxicated by inordinate amounts of rum or cold Crystal beer.

That night I was introduced to Tiny on the door at El Gato Tuerto. Of course, with a name like that he was massive; great fists like hams and a smile just as big. A former Olympic boxer, he practises his chops tending door at El Gato. I don't suppose even the most rum-soaked patron gives Tiny much trouble.

As we embraced and were then ushered into the darkness inside like important and powerful guests, I realised this was part of Havana's tidal pull. You feel like you're in a Raymond Chandler movie; trailing the bad guy, drinking with molls, using your contacts and savvy to work your way around this crumbling city, always trying to work just under the surface to find the best spots and the coolest people.

It was pitch-dark inside, the bar packed and on stage was someone special. I can almost guarantee it'll be the same when you go. It may be a famous Cuban pianist or a sensational up and coming young singer. Just grab a table or somewhere you can stand if there are none available – and watch the night disappear like a swirl of smoke.

Around three in the morning, a band took to the stage and kicked off with a set of turbo-charged Cuban classics. It's not just tourists here, you see. Friday is a big night in Havana, as it is anywhere, and the locals go big with it. There was dancing – plenty of fast, frenzied, sensual dancing. And singing too, the band playing up to the audience and inviting them to crash in on well-known Cuban hits. The musicians were sensational and that night there was a beautiful girl in a little black number playing an absurdly cool saxophone.

As she segued into a mesmerising reggae intro, I let my gaze drift across the room. Arms were in the air, bodies were swaying and there was a sense of euphoria that's difficult to describe. The saxophonist clung seductively to her sparkling instrument, her hips seemingly having a life independent of the rest of her body – then she soared into 'No Woman No Cry'. I turned to my brothers in arms and we were all grinning at each other inanely. It's a moment I'll never forget.

Now it's the morning after the night before. And I'm watching the fisherman and trying not to think about the crashing cymbals now playing in my head.

The downside to days and nights in Cuba is the gradual erosion of your motor and mental faculties. On the first morning here, I was up early, brimming with enthusiasm to make the most of my trip. I'm staying in a bay-side villa, complete with pool and a view across a usually tranquil sea from a canopied dining area and bar. Perfect.

The rest of my housemates are out and about or sleeping off the jet lag, and after a to-and-fro pigeon-English conversation with our lovely Cuban hostess and a slightly bizarre breakfast – a croissant, a coffee and a fried egg served on a lonely plate of its own – I've determined roughly where we are and how to get back in one piece, and I'm out the door.

Of course, it's hot. A hat is essential. As are collared shirts and decent shorts. Make sure there's some stomach trouble pills and toilet tissue in your pocket, alongside some Cuban Convertible Dollars (CUCs). Now you are fixed for exploration Havana style. Oh – and don't forget the sunglasses. Your forthcoming headache will be grateful.

Sprawling blocks of habitation – some proudly kept, others in a ramshackle state of disrepair – form the urban outskirts of this great city. At once, you feel safe to wander the streets. Tourists keep this island ticking and if a Cuban is caught messing with one, it's a serious crime indeed.

Folks give you a stare, but it's inquisitive rather than adversarial. If you nod and raise a hand with a *'Buenos dias'* you'll likely get the same in reply. Obligatory scabby dogs scratch and snooze in the gutters. Dilapidated cars bounce around potholes.

Within a street or so I'm sweating and the blue suede loafers I've bought are already scraping one heel raw. I navigate the streets, passing fruit stalls and bars consisting of little more than a few plastic chairs. I try to remember the way home, while giving the impression of being a well-travelled Havana expert.

Eventually I hit Fifth Avenue, the arterial dual carriageway which runs through the heart of the city, and stroll back on myself, past bus stops of dark stares and over rusting bridges revealing tantalising glimpses of brackish water beneath.

By the time I find 'our' street once more, I'm dripping with sweat. The humidity is close to 100 per cent. My ankle is leaving bloodied stripes across the back of my short sock as I limp across the threshold. I haven't distinguished myself first crack out of the box – but my passion hasn't dimmed.

The following days run to a later and later timescale as the hours logged in bars and clubs add up, but I maintain my enthusiasm. For most of the time, at least.

Official cigar events can be painful, if truth be known. Habanos SA holds several during the week, and while, if they were offered in isolation at any other time they would be welcomed, in a week of meetings, tastings, catch-ups and late nights they can become a trial.

Food at these events isn't the best, to put it politely, although it's improved beyond all recognition since my first trip to cigar heaven. No, the best fun is to be had once you've slipped away from the official gathering and found a welcoming bar nearby. You never have to look too far. Then cold beers slake the thirst, your cigars are welcomed without question and you can chat the night away with the assortment of characters you collect on such trips.

As ever, I'm in good company. The Fox family of Dublin bought London's legendary Robert Lewis cigar store back in the mid-1990s, but they've been involved in the cigar business and more for a lot longer. There's a book in the family story alone.

As well as their other interests in Jersey, the Foxes now run the famous old store on St James's Street, London, as well as a luxurious cigar offering within the deeps of Harrods in Knightsbridge and in Selfridges of Bond Street. There's a host of cigar experts under their roof, ready, willing and able to assist. And the Fox keeps are something to behold.

Cigar keeps or vaults are where the treasure lies. Because cigars have to be both temperature and climate-controlled, English specialist retailers were among the first in the world to set up dedicated rooms to ensure stocks were kept in the finest possible condition. London's cigar emporia therefore began to 'lay down' prime cigar stocks for their most discerning customers. Just like fine wine – or myself, for that matter – great tobacco can both improve in flavour and complexity with age. Those in the know chose – and still choose – their favoured sticks and laid them down with the intention of smoking them years later at something close to their peak.

The result, among the best of London's cigar keeps, is the aforementioned treasure: box after box of sought-after sizes; shelf after shelf of limited-edition humidors, discontinued lines, rarities and ancient glories.

The keep at J J Fox is one such.

It's out of bounds to the public, unlike the rest of the sprawling townhouse on the hill of St James's Street where you can sit in Churchill's favourite armchair or peruse Oscar Wilde's unpaid tobacco bills. It's dark, chilly and sepulchral in the vaults. Old wooden cabinets of great vintages loom up at you out of the dark; lost names are scrawled on stickers on shelves to depict ownership.

These names drift through the room like Scrooge's apparitions: old politicians, peers, long-dead Home Secretaries, modern-day screen stars and more. These boxes – worth many millions of pounds – are held in the strictest of confidence. So strict, in fact, that sometimes a decades-old inventory is held without knowing exactly who the rightful owner is. The original buyer dies and leaves his mighty cigar collection behind – but the family, presumably not knowing that he had them or at least what they are worth – never get in touch.

The unscrupulous cigar merchant would, of course, cover his arse by making a token effort to 'find' those due the inheritance – and then sell them himself at massive profit. Not so here.

These names drift through the room like Scrooge's apparitions: old politicians, peers, long-dead Home Secretaries, modern-day screen stars and more.

'We don't know who owns some of the old, old stock,' admits Rob Fox as we stretch our legs and try to catch that elusive Havana warm breeze that still stands in for air conditioning in many of the city's establishments.

This is no ordinary Italian restaurant – there are pictures on the wall of visits from Mick Jagger and Robert de Niro – and there's an unmistakeable charge of electricity in the air, despite the relaxing vibes. Cuba is like that; it's inherently exciting, and I'm not sure why.

Rob is one of life's observers – piercing brown eyes behind glasses give him a hawkish expression and he tends to listen rather than to talk until he gets to know you. His brother Stuart is the extrovert of the family (and he doesn't seem to sleep, either, I can tell you from bleary-eyed experience). He is not a man renowned for sitting still in one place for any great length of time.

Together they run the Fox family's cigar enterprise and having been to Havana scores of times over the years, they have got travelling around the city down to a fine art.

You're only as good as your man on the ground in Cuba; as mentioned earlier, you need to know where to meet and with whom. After painstaking research – and, one suspects, plenty of trial and error – the Foxes are now able to swerve the worst of it.

It's 'their' seaside villa I'm staying at which allows me to observe the foam boat diver, and this afternoon – post-headache, thank God – I'm enjoying lunch with them at a 'little Italian place' they know of. It's here, over cold beers and a superb aubergine starter (eggplant for my American friends) that I learn of J J Fox's 'lost treasure'.

'We've had people come in and ask about long-forgotten stock – and sometimes we've been able to pull out the old ledgers and track them down. It's come as quite a shock to some of them.'

I can imagine. The chances of my being left a horde of long-forgotten, well-kept cigars is slim to none, but nevertheless...

Rob digs into his backpack and pulls out an obviously old cigar box. It's a box of Partagas, a well-known and loved Cuban brand, the labels peeling, the cedar wood yellow with age. There's no specific *vitola*, or size information, which is unusual as it's normally printed on the box. And from the box information and handwritten annotations, Rob has worked out these particular beauties are from before 1954.

Just take a second to imagine what water under the bridge there has been around the world since the fateful day this humble little cigar was born.

I take one reverentially – I'm always a little embarrassed at cigar folks' generosity, especially when it involves lifetime-memory moments, like this one. I stammer my profound thanks, repeatedly ask: 'Are you sure?' and take a closer look at the box. That's when I get a jolt as I read what's written on one side.

Instead of the normal size name – Corona, Robusto, Churchill or similar – there are two simple words printed here. Stratford House.

I get a jolt because I recognise this name. I'm undoubtedly the only person in Cuba right now who would.

'I've no idea what or where Stratford House is,' says Rob cheerfully as he fires up his 64-year-old plus cigar.

'I have,' I say, staring at the box.

The rest of the table looks up.

Stratford House, you see, holds a special place in my heart. I doubt you've heard of it and I doubt even if you walk down Oxford Street every day of your life you've even seen it. It exists seemingly within its own little magic bubble – and it's my home from home in London.

Stratford House is also the home of the Oriental Club – one of the country's oldest and most distinguished private members' clubs. Now, I've learned that the moment one mentions private members' clubs, there is potential for snobbery. While I understand Clubland can lead to gaudy images of landed toffs propping up bars when they should be working, the truth is, as always, never as black and white.

Some of these great old institutions are the last remaining bastions of traditional, formal hospitality in the best and least snobby of its guises. The very fact that clubs exist where only members are allowed seems to infuriate some. To me, this seems eminently sensible. Why form a club of like-minded people if it's likely to be spoiled by others of a different point of view? Each to his own, I say. Even my local village working men's club – which is equally hospitable in its own way – has a membership procedure.

I digress. The Oriental Club was founded in 1824 by the Duke of Wellington and his friends on return from their travails in the East. It has been frequented by military men, peers, scholars and characters ever since.

Described by Charles Dickens as being 'composed of noblemen, MPs and gentleman of the first character', little has changed in the intervening years. Except that I too may occasionally be found pottering its corridors.

Richard Terry, the Oriental Club's original *chef de cuisine*, published the seminal *Indian Cookery* in 1861, one of the first of its kind in the country to detail how to cook curries. A copy of the book still sits in one corner of the Calcutta Light Horse Bar where one can enjoy a plate of oysters or a taste of Indian street food. Just along the corridor is the Dining Room, which is another major draw for members. There are two full-time Indian chefs, a tandoor oven in the kitchen and a daily Eastern menu – vindaloo pork cheek, anyone? – to sit alongside club favourites like potted shrimp and roast beef and Yorkshire pud. There's just enough British eccentricity here to make this a vibrant, joyous place to be. You can pop your shoes outside your door at night and they'll be returned polished in the early hours. And there's also a ram's head in the Smoking Room (sadly no longer smoking), which contains snuff you can scoop out with a silver spoon.

Wonderfully batty.

But Havana is a long way from that little cul-de-sac opposite Bond Street Tube station, where traffic and shoppers are swept along one of the world's busiest shopping streets like flotsam on a swollen river.

As I light up this old, lightly perfumed cigar, I feel humbled. To be able to enjoy such a cigar with such history, in such company and such surroundings truly is a blessing.

I can tell you that the hour or so it took me to smoke that cigar had something of a dreamlike quality, as did the rest of that afternoon, as a matter of fact. I felt a little like I was floating on air for the rest of the day.

> **As I light up this old, lightly perfumed cigar, I feel humbled. To be able to enjoy such a cigar with such history, in such company and such surroundings truly is a blessing.**

Old cigars can be terrible: over-aged ones have this clagging, nauseating *perfumed* quality that once tasted, is never forgotten. But if kept well and if having been made of good, strong tobacco in the first place, old cigars can be ethereal. Age slowly mellows them; rounds sharp edges; adds mystique and nuance to blends; gives a long finish a wistful tang.

My thanks to the Fox brothers and the Oriental Club for that other-worldly smoke. And also to the memory of that long-ago cigar roller extraordinaire who, one day back in 1954, rolled a humble cigar that would make its way around the world to the vaults of a London club; and yet would find its way home to be smoked in 2018. That just blows me away.

Dawn in Cuba is as unmistakably beautiful as it is anywhere else in the world.

There's a blessed coolness in the air, one which you know will dissipate in double-quick time as soon as the sun rises and ruffles its feathers. A soft breeze moves the tropical foliage, and exotic birds, excited to be on the forage for another day, hop and call among the fronds.

As previously explained, night-time revels mean that the chances of you seeing a Cuban dawn are limited mainly to seeing it through bleary eyes as you stumble home to bed.

Not, though, if your name is Laurence Davis.

For Davis, as previously mentioned, is the charismatic owner of Sautter Cigars, a highly regarded London cigar store on Mayfair's prestigious Mount Street, directly opposite The Connaught hotel. He is an early bird.

Sautter was opened by the much-loved and much-missed Desmond Sautter in the 1960s and he had the foresight to build the UK's first walk-in humidor. Laurence, a property magnate with a string of business interests, was a long-time customer of Desmond's (and presumably a very profitable one, given his vast capacity for cigars) and when Des decided the time was right to retire, it was Laurence who finally persuaded him to sell.

Since then, Laurence – or 'El Jeffe' as he's often known within the walls of Sautters – has strode the cigar world like a colossus. His enthusiasm for Cuban cigars is unbounded. As is his capacity to smoke them.

He won't thank me for telling you this, as Mrs D is kept somewhat in the dark as to exact details, but by his own admission, Laurence is an 'industrial cigar smoker'. From the moment he opens his peepers to the moment he closes them again, a great fat Cuban cigar is never far away from lip or hand.

Which is why, in Cuba, if you are capable of rising early to greet the cool dawn (and it is a wonderful way to see a different face of this marvellous country) you may well bump into Laurence sitting by the pool.

It'll be 5.30 or 6 a.m. and he'll already be plugged in and turned on; laptop on the go, mobile handset by his side; a huge hard case of cigars nearby and ashtrays, lighters and cutters deftly daubed in circumference around him. Even at this tender hour of the day, he'll have a cigar on the go. Generally speaking, it will be roughly of the same dimensions as a North American Redwood tree. Laurence isn't one for subtle undertones.

We've known each other for years and have recently started recording a series of Sautter video reviews for a bit of fun. They've proved something of a hit, with tens of thousands of viewers tuning in to watch us talk cigars and an awful lot of rubbish besides.

On my last visit to Cuba, I toured with L D himself.

My morning started just as described. Going against previous form, I was actually in bed before midnight and was able to rise and see the purple blush of morning sunrise from the villa we were sharing.

Of course, I couldn't beat El Jeffe to the breakfast table. He was sitting there, smouldering, like a large, omnipotent cigar-smelling Buddha, by the time I poked my bed head around the door. After a dip in the cold pool, which refreshed the parts other pools can't reach, I was able to join him and one of my most memorable cigar days had begun.

Breakfast in Cuba, as I've already said, is a bit hit and miss. Past experience has taught me the error of my ways, so now I am exacting in my demands: a small plate of fruit, a cup of strong black coffee and a three-egg omelette with a sprinkle of cheese. Done.

Today, after breakfast, Laurence and I are heading west. It's time for another trip to the renowned Pinar del Río and this time we have an appointment with a master.

Alejandro Robaina was possibly the greatest cigar-leaf grower of all time. His legendary small finca deep in the heart of Pinar del Río grew to legendary status due to the extraordinary quality of large wrapper leaf it continues to grow.

Nowhere else could match this beautiful leaf and its deep, complex array of Cuban flavours. Robaina became a pin-up for the Cuban cigar industry. He was feted by Fidel Castro, permitted to travel worldwide to promote Habanos brands. Eventually he was awarded a brand of his own and his instantly recognisable face – lined with an incredible set of wrinkles – was synonymous with Cuban tobacco. He lived until he was ninety-one and spent the vast majority of his life on the few small acres of his beloved farm, spending hours in his dotage sitting in his rocking chair and smoking a home-rolled cigar.

It is to my lasting regret that I never got to meet Don Alejandro. I knew of him, of course, and longed for nothing more than the opportunity to sit with him in one of his famous rocking chairs on the verandah of Finca Robaina and shoot the breeze. Alas, I never made it. But today, I'm going to put that right.

Alejandro's grandson, Hiroshi, was handpicked from eleven grandchildren to be the one to carry on the master's legacy. He's still not quite sure why.

'He saw something in me,' he says and his rocking chair squeaks gently. I've finally made it to that verandah. All around me is the greenery of the world's best tobacco and today there's a lump in my throat I can't quite shift.

'To this day, I'm not sure why, but he told me that I had the feel for it. And he began to teach me.'

Back then, Hiroshi would sit in these very same chairs and write down every word the old man said to him. Book after book of cigar lore; priceless; unknown; probably unteachable unless you happened to be a blood relative.

> All around me is the greenery of the world's best tobacco and today there's a lump in my throat I can't quite shift.

Weather, seasons, varieties, techniques, telltale signs, problems, solutions, ideas – a lifetime's work distilled into a young man desperate not to let his *abuelo* down.

It's a touching tale and as Hiroshi recounts it in his broken English, there's no disguising the emotion in his voice as he talks about his mentor, now long gone and still missed every single day.

There's a wooden statue of Don Alejandro at the farm, made from a single huge block of cedar wood. It's incredibly lifelike, even down to those trademark wrinkles, and it's a life-size rendition of the old master in his rocking chair, complete with cigar in hand. It keeps catching the corner of your eye and you can't help getting the slightly ghostly feeling that he's still there keeping an eye on proceedings.

And somehow, I think that's the point of having the statue there. During a quiet moment after our verandah interview, Hiroshi quite naturally pulls up the chair next to his grandfather, lights a cigar and relaxes back. He

reaches out and his hand subconsciously descends over the wooden one of the old man. As far as he's concerned, no one is watching and it's a perfectly natural manoeuvre. He just sits peacefully, smoking and holding hands with his grandfather.

Like all Cuban tobacco men, money is hard to come by for Hiroshi. He's better off than most, for his farm is internationally renowned, and visitors often bring him gifts and basic items from abroad.

But he and his young family still live in a way we in the West can barely imagine. We're lucky enough to share their lunch today – chicken, rice, beans and coffee – all of it grown right here on the farm. It's simple all right, but utterly delicious. The chicken is unlike any bland supermarket fare you've ever tasted and the rich strong coffee as fresh and invigorating as a rain-fed shower.

And of course, smoking a cigar here is similarly stimulating. A selection of dark, alluring beauties lie on the tabletop before us and while El Jeffe chooses one more or less the size of a telegraph pole, I select a long, slender number, which immediately results in voluble comparisons to my manhood.

Shrugging off such slurs, I light up following my divine lunch and kick back to enjoy one of those cigar moments that will remain with me all my life. There's something immensely spiritual about this quiet place. Chickens scratch and squabble; dogs sleep in the dust. Old machinery coughs, roars into life, dies again. And silence reigns over a hot, fertile countryside that produces an unequally vast percentage of the world's best cigars.

I sit with Laurence and, for once, the banter is quiet, the small talk unnecessary. We both know this is something special and we don't spoil it with banal conversation. Just the rustle of leaves, the trill of a bird and the call of one farm worker to another.

CHAPTER SEVEN

New World and Cuban

ACQUIRE NEW KNOWLEDGE WHILST THINKING OVER THE OLD,
AND YOU MAY BECOME A TEACHER OF OTHERS.

— Confucius

There's a distinction in hand-rolled cigars, clear for all to see. Those that are Cuban – and those that aren't.

Non-Cuban – or New World – cigars have exploded on the scene. As little as fifteen years ago, they were virtually unheard of outside the US. Today, they are marching ever onwards over what was once hallowed 'Cuban-only' territory.

Money from US-based manufacturers has flooded into countries like Nicaragua (the fastest growing New World producer of them all) and built state-of-the-art factories; been invested in fertiliser and irrigation solutions; created agronomy labs and disease-resistant hybrids.

Ironically, while Cuba may remain the best geographically positioned of all the world's countries to grow cigar tobacco, its state-owned cigar operation cannot compete with the funding and the innovation of the New World. While accurate information about Cuba's cigar economy is notoriously difficult to obtain, it is fair to say that money for fertilisers, modern farm machinery and access to adequate laboratories is thin on the ground. And this is where the New World has come in.

Names like Joya de Nicaragua, Padrón, Drew Estate, Alec Bradley, Rocky Patel, La Flor Dominicana, My Father Cigars: these are now all household names in cigar circles. And none of them feature Cuban tobacco – yet.

The Cuban cigar industry is based on tradition – old houses or *marques* with centuries of heritage behind them. Some lines have been sold in the same format for donkey's years.

This is both good and bad.

Good, because tobacco husbandry is in the blood of Cubans; there is no nation on earth better at dealing with tobacco, for none have the experience the Cubans have gathered. Lore and practical guidance have been passed down from factory to factory and from patriarch to patriarch through the generations, and this knowledge – this mostly unwritten tobacco *interpretation* – is quite simply priceless.

I wonder if the powers that be in Cuba adequately realise this. That the industry that makes one of the world's greatest luxury products has very little to do with old factories or plantations of tobacco; it isn't about machinery, or the fancy names, marketing or the intricate bands it puts on its cigars. It's about people. They hold the secret to Cuban tobacco and its ongoing success.

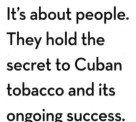

It's about people. They hold the secret to Cuban tobacco and its ongoing success.

Because of this knowledge, growing, curing, selecting, blending, rolling and ageing cigars in Cuba is second to none when it's done right.

Have you ever had a truly sensational bottle of French wine and, upon sipping it, realised that the stars have aligned, it is utterly sublime and beyond improvement? If you are lucky enough to get a magnificent example of Cuban cigar making, this is how you might feel. A wonderful Cuban cigar is an ephemeral, life-enhancing, enchanting, memorable experience.

But they're not all like that by any stretch.

Lack of investment and, frankly, a sometimes spotty approach to quality control, mean that Cuban cigars suffer more burning and drawing defects than New World cigars.

Why such a discrepancy? New World cigars have had to sell themselves on quality and reliability rather than history and prestige. Ask any New World manufacturer (and I have) and they will tell you that poorly made cigars – cigars that won't draw properly (meaning it's difficult to obtain a clear flow of air through them), cigars that are blended or rolled imperfectly so that they burn crookedly, affecting the taste – would simply not be tolerated in their markets.

The majority of major New World cigar makers are based – or at least have a foothold in – the United States, for this is the largest cigar market in the world. Americans are used to service – used to buying goods that do what they say they'll do, time after time. They expect their favourite drinks, their favourite snacks, their favourite *cigars*, to taste the same, each and every time they reach for them.

Over the years, Cuban smokers have learned to deal with the occasional plugged or poorly blended cigar with a shrug of the shoulders; this is Cuba, they say. We pay for the extraordinary smokes that Cuba offers with the blood of their fallen brethren who weren't quite up to the job.

In America, the reputation of the business is on the line with each and every stick sold.

No one better exemplifies this difference in approach than Padrón. It's a super-premium hand-rolled cigar from Nicaragua, created by the remark-able Don José Padrón, who sadly recently passed away after an extraordinary lifetime in cigars. I've been fortunate enough to sit with his son, Jorgé, on the family veranda in Estelí, Nicaragua. He told me, as cars honked and streetlights cast a flare across the night sky, that *every single Padrón cigar must be perfect.*

'We would be out of business if we didn't have a strict policy of quality control,' he said as we smoked sensational unbanded Padrón 80th Anniversary cigars from his humidor and drank warming Nicaraguan rum.

'Americans would be knocking our door down, demanding their money back. They can go and spend that money on another New World cigar, they don't have to stick with Padrón if we don't satisfy them. That's the difference between us and Cuba.'

Many of the men and women behind New World blends such as Padrón started out their cigar lives in the hallowed Cuban tobacco fields. But when their plantations and farms were nationalised after Fidel Castro's Revolu-tion, they felt they had no choice other than to leave the country and begin anew elsewhere.

They found new and fertile tobacco plains in Honduras, in Dominican Republic and in Nicaragua. And they've since created successful cigar busi-nesses of their own once again.

This doesn't mean they have given up on their ancestral homes. Far from it. Many US-based cigar makers (and there's a bunch of them based in Miami, just ninety miles north of Havana) still fiercely treasure the thought of one day returning to their homeland.

At the time of writing, Castro has finally hung up his standard-issue Army boots and marched through the pearly gates. There has been some rapprochement between feuding Cuban ex-pats and the government and a slight loosening on the iron grip that has held the Cuban people for so long.

But we are no closer to solving the problem of repatriating former owners with their State-seized goods and land. And that's without beginning to scratch the surface of Cuban brands that were resurrected elsewhere with New World tobacco. This admittedly confusing state of affairs means that there is a Cuban Montecristo – and one made in the Dominican Republic. The two – from a perspective of branding and packaging – are indistinguishable to the untrained eye. This also applies to well-known Cuban brands such as Partagás, Romeo y Julieta, Punch, El Rey Del Mundo and more. So, who legitimately owns the brand and its worldwide distribution rights? How does one side compensate the other?

One day, these matters will have their time in court and a resolution will be made by a judge. There may be a financial settlement; it would have to come from a very large pot. But for the time being – and it was ever thus – the only ones getting rich are the lawyers.

New World manufacturers have to pay more attention to QC then – but they have a blank slate when it comes to marketing their products. Some follow the tradition of well-placed advertisements in the cigar press, featuring family members in tobacco fields or in curing barns, sniffing fermenting leaf and looking old, wise and knowledgeable. Others shy away from tradition and instead look to shake up the cosy, old-school-tie image.

Jonathan Drew is indubitably one of the most radical thinkers and manipulators in the cigar world in the last twenty years. J D – just one of the many monikers he calls himself – is no ordinary cigar maker. He's as likely to rock up in baggy shorts and red-tinted glasses, dripping with jewellery, and with a slew of ideas. It's safe to say, he's not short of a word or two, either.

He's a New Yorker with an attitude (come to think of it, is there such a thing as a New Yorker *without* an attitude?) and he launched Drew Estate with partner Marvin Samel in a tiny kiosk in the World Trade Centre. They were pals, they loved cigars, they decided to make some.

Except that their entry into the cigar market was perfectly timed to coincide with that very market's collapse. In the early nineties, a positive boom had taken place, resulting in a flood of new manufacturers entering the fray and finding easy and lucrative markets for their cigars.

But when there's a boom, there's always a bust. And it was sinking in as Drew and Samel were taking their first tentative steps.

J D moved to Estelí in 1998 – then little more than an outpost in northern Nicaragua, which was still recovering from years of bitter civil conflict. The cigar boom years had helped re-establish Nicaragua as a cigar-making nation and Estelí itself as a cigar town, but it was still a brave or foolhardy move for a New Yorker to arrive and try to get on side with the host of families and tobacco men who had seen an awful lot of other supposed cigar makers come and go.

They called him 'El Gringo Loco' – the Crazy Foreigner. He slept on a mattress in a crummy old factory and didn't speak a whole lot of Spanish. That's J D for you.

But he persevered and Drew Estate today is one of the biggest cigar makers on the planet. It's certainly one of Estelí's largest employers and it's no exaggeration to say that locals are queuing up to work there.

The massive factory has to be seen to be believed. Walking into the salon de torcido in Estelí is something you'll never forget. There are circa 800 rollers rattling through their work. *800.* You will never see so many rollers under one roof again in your life.

You'll have to talk loudly to whoever is with you. Chavetas (the odd curved knives used to cut tobacco) bang on the rolling tables, which stretch for yards and yards across the massive room. People are everywhere, picking up their tobacco, shifting newly rolled cigars, swapping shifts. It's a special place.

If you're lucky and you're with J D, he'll grab a stick that's just been rolled, fresh from the table, and hand it to you with a glint in his eye. For there's nothing on God's green earth – nothing I tell you – like the taste of a freshly rolled cigar right there in the factory.

If you've taken a tour to Drew Estate, you must also visit Joya de Nicaragua while in the country. This is a no-brainer, as the kids might say.

You'll soon see it's nothing like the behemoth cousin up the road. But what it lacks in size, it makes up for in character and history. For Joya de Nicaragua is the father factory – or mother, if you prefer – for the whole of the Central American country. It was the first to be specifically built to manufacture cigars and, indeed, its early cigars were the first from the country to be exported.

I was fortunate enough to be asked by Joya to write a history of the company to celebrate its recent fiftieth anniversary, so it – and more specifically, its people – holds a special place in my heart. *Cinco Décadas: The Rise of the Nicaraguan Cigar*, as the subsequent book was called, recounts the incredible history of this little factory on the outskirts of Estelí, from its humble beginnings with its original founders, to being owned by despised dictator Somoza, through terrible years of bloodshed and warfare, revolution and destruction.

During the research for this, I spent some time in Nicaragua speaking to those with a grip on its turbulent history: historians, writers, poets, tobacco men, learned men and women who had lived through the storms to see beyond to peace. It's a humbling tale of greed and redemption, and some of the men and women who ply their trade at the Joya factory have done so since the beginning – fifty years ago.

Their loyalty is staggering. Some of them walked to work while fighter planes roared overhead to drop bombs: they avoided bodies caught up in overnight fighting, dived for cover when gunmen opened fire in broad daylight. They weren't paid for months on end; one time their factory was set alight *while they were inside*. It was reported that when government forces had taken control of the building, people were executed upstairs.

Despite the horror of its history, today there is no hint of the sinister at Joya de Nicaragua. Instead, it's a place of light and laughter, of friendship and joined purpose.

Quite aside its propensities as a great cigar-making nation,

Nicaragua is also an incredible country to visit. You can peep over the rim of a volcano and literally see the boiling lava roiling and flowing below you. I know, because I've done it.

With pristine beaches on both Caribbean and Pacific sides of the country, rich rainforest between and an astonishing wealth of bird, insect, mammal and reptilian life, it's a country of breathtaking freshness, even today. Although foreign interests wielding thick bundles of dollars are working hard to take advantage of these riches for their own ends. The US government has played a particularly heavy-handed part in Nicaragua's history.

In the northern province of Matagalpa, the jungle lies thick and tortuous roads ascend to the cool foothills of mountains shrouded in mist. I arrive at Selva Negra after darkness has fallen, exhausted after a day of travel and interview, and ready for my rest. A stiff breeze shifts through unseen foliage as I am shown to my chalet.

There is a back light on. And the biggest cloud of moths and insects I've ever seen in my life. There is every shape and colour too, from huge, flapping, handkerchief-sized specimens to thumbnail-sized, brightly hued beauties. And in order to reach the sanctuary of my room, I have to wade through them.

Too tired to care, I nip in as fast as I could and even then a moth and a couple of dozen of his mates slip in and continue their party in the rafters. The place is spotless and a quick brush of the teeth and change and I am ready to slip between the sheets and sleep the sleep of the righteous. Until I see the spider in the corner of the bedroom.

It isn't huge. I'm not going to exaggerate just for effect. It is of small to medium size, to be perfectly accurate in my description. It's just that it is *chunky*.

It is indeed too chunky to be just another medium-sized spider. It had that heft of leg; that plumpness of body; that overall coiled-spring articulatedness about its multiple limbs that in all honesty scream of *tarantula*.

This is a term that we, in the UK at least, have coined to mark those large hairy exotic species of spider that we only dream about in our worst nightmares. In England, the biggest spiders we get are great gangly rapid beasties that come in from the fields at harvest time and leg it across the lounge carpet when you are least expecting it. They are certainly not tarantulas.

I was a boy brought up on Johnny Weissmuller's old black-and-white Tarzan series; on James Bond in tales of derring-do in sunny Jamaica. These would feature the fantastic black tarantulas of my imagination.

In adulthood, I've learned to curb my irrational fear, to help my children overcome theirs. But I'll still admit to a creeping sense of panic when a spider comes in very close proximity.

And now, within a shoe's throw of my bed, is what I would describe as a small tarantula. Great.

I am so tired and I know I just need to sleep. I can't call reception, because it isn't manned overnight; there's just a security guard keeping tabs on the place. And the thought of standing in the dark waiting for him, then trying to get him to understand I am out here in the middle of the night because of a spider in my room is too much to contemplate. So, I slip gingerly into bed and force myself not to look directly at my new arachnid friend in the periphery of my vision, although he remains there like an ink blot on my consciousness.

I pick up my Kindle and began to read. Or pretend to read. My eyes scan the words on the electronic reader, but my brain does not compute them. In its overtired state, it is acting on autopilot, conjuring scenarios and situations and rolling them into a David Lynchian concoction of craziness. I shut my eyes. It's time to take a grip. I need to sleep, I have no intention of trying to tackle the hairy beastie and throw him outside (and there is an army of moths waiting to come in anyway), so we have to put up with each other.

Still without looking at him and while appearing to be absorbed in the book I am currently reading (Thomas Belt's ancient *Naturalist in Nicaragua*, helpfully enough) I say aloud: 'Let's make a deal. You leave me alone, and I'll leave you alone, okay?'

The spider doesn't answer. But in all honesty, I hadn't expected him to. I put in earplugs, pull on an eye mask, turn over and switch off the light.

He is gone in the morning.

Whither to, I never find out, although I pay particular attention to my shoes and to the bag at the end of my bed. And the moths had decamped, too, presumably to sleep off their hangovers from headbanging against my window all night.

The morning is fresh and clear and glorious. Before me lies mile after mile of virgin forest, unseen in the blackness of the night before. Pale morning sunshine creeps across the horizon and vultures circle lazily. Coffee bushes spring from the very slopes beyond my cabin. These aren't what you'd expect, actually; they're spindly, puny looking plants with a few haphazard branches spilling left and right. I bend to pick the bright red berry of a coffee fruit.

Selva Negra grows some of Nicaragua's finest coffee. It's the perfect altitude, with cool nights and humid days. And here on the resort and farm run by Eddie Kühl and his tireless wife, Mausi, several hundred workers at a time gather to tend and ultimately harvest the precious crop.

> The morning is fresh and clear and glorious. Before me lies mile after mile of virgin forest, unseen in the blackness of the night before.

It's a remarkable operation from the family, whose origins are in Germany (hence Selva Negra, or 'Black Forest'). After turning his engineering prowess into building and maintaining things like the turbine on the lake, which provides electricity to the farm, and the solar panels on the roof of my cabin, Eddie Kühl has taken it upon himself to write several books on Nicaragua and its people. He sits with me in the shade of the restaurant overlooking the water-lily-spotted lake and we talk through a humid morning.

'My people came here from Germany with the promise of a new life,' he says. 'There were posters at Hamburg train station promising land for a dollar an acre. And many came and set up home. And they found it was perfect for growing coffee.'

Nicaraguan coffee is prized. Selva Negra harvests and roasts its own, as well as running eco lodges, a resort and a full working farm. If you ever find yourself here, it's well worth taking a tour. The indomitable Mausi took me on a whistlestop version the morning after the spider incident. She's a tiny powerhouse, keeping tabs on the entire operation and looking after the hundreds of workers who may be on the farm at any one time. There is a huge amount going on here – a farm and slaughterhouse to provide meat for the restaurant, polytunnels and gardens to grow fresh fruit and veg, innovative waste recycling, water purification system and perhaps best of all, the protection of a Nature Reserve that runs into thousands of acres of precious mountain jungle housing myriad birds and animals.

It's a constant battle to keep the jungle from reclaiming its own. Add to that the complexity of employing people on such a scale and in such a rural environment; the various factions that, from time to time in Nicaraguan history, have taken refuge in these mountains and threatened the safety of the enclave; and the sheer difficulty of running modern machinery in such an outpost – all of these add up to what your average human being would consider odds beyond reckoning. But Eddie Kühl, Mausi and their family are not average human beings.

They recognise the need to care for their land for the next generation, while making it pay its way – and keeping a roof over the heads of scores of families – at the same time. Selva Negra is fantastic, and I urge you to support it. There aren't many places like it left in the world.

Estelí was once your classic one-horse town.

Even now, *vaqueros*, or cowboys are found, lounging against buildings and adjusting their ten-gallon hats or admiring their *vaquero* boots. If you head out into the sticks, you'll see plenty more of them, and as an added bonus, they'll likely be on horseback to complete the picture.

In Estelí, the Mitsubishi 4x4 has overtaken the horse as the *vaquero* transport of choice. Shame. The clop of horses is infinitely more pleasurable than the heaving churn of traffic in Estelí, but if I lived here, I'd want one too.

Chickens still wander around on the outskirts of town, an obligatory scabby dog can be found napping in the middle of a quiet street. As I wander down a sultry street at noontime, a vulture eyes me menacingly from an overhead telephone pole.

As I wander down a sultry street at noontime, a vulture eyes me menacingly from an overhead telephone pole.

None of the above is designed to patronise the city; it's a city with rural charm and long may it stay that way. The people of Estelí are a breed of their own: fiercely independent, fiercely loyal, they stick together in extended families and have, for generations, born the brunt of Nicaragua's tumultuous past with fortitude.

And they've also manned Estelí's growth into the biggest tobacco town in the world.

Factories are built here regularly. As well as Padròn, Joya de Nicaragua and Drew Estate, there's scores of others, small, medium and large. A J Fernandez has built a whopping great facility stretching for several blocks. The Fuente family, makers of world-famous Dominican cigars, plan a triumphant return to Nicaragua after being forced out during the Revolution of the late 1970s and early 1980s.

As a result of this cigar money – largely from US entrepreneurs – schools and clinics have sprung up. Cigar makers on the whole are humanitarians, and the standard of living in Estelí has risen considerably among cigar workers. It's why jobs at these factories are continually oversubscribed.

Tax incentives have also helped the cigar industry here grow bigger than that in Cuba. It's key to the continued success and rise from poverty that the industry continues to thrive and support its loyal workers.

CHAPTER EIGHT

Great White Shark

"SIGH NO MORE, LADIES, SIGH NO MORE, MEN WERE
DECEIVERS EVER –
ONE FOOT IN SEA AND ONE ON SHORE,
TO ONE THING CONSTANT NEVER."

— *William Shakespeare*

'What would you do if you had no fear?'

That was the question I asked my pal Wal one Friday night over a pint in our local.

'Eh?' he replied, lucidly.

I was young and dumb and determined not to slouch through life, but to grab it by the short and curlies and make it howl. I had a lot to learn.

'Come on; there must be things you would like to do but are too afraid to try,' I said. 'Hang-gliding, scuba-diving, dating a ginger girl…'

We talked it over that Friday night. It was a five-pint problem, I reckon, involving much incredulity and no small amount of laughing. And then I remember saying: 'Diving with great white sharks,' with drunken finality, draining the last amber liquid from my pint pot and slamming it down on the table in a foamy thud.

Wal looked at me, thunderstruck. He's got somewhat used to my occasionally wild outbursts over the years, and he always has a look to see if I'm joking or not. I wasn't.

Normally these daft conversations are forgotten as soon as we stagger home and collapse into bed to dream and perchance to snore. Not this one, though, due, I think, to my stubborn internal insistence that I really should give it a try.

Like many of us, the subconscious image of the great white had haunted me since childhood. I was fascinated with all wildlife as a child and would spend hours poring over an old natural history book that was gathering dust on the family bookshelf. It was titled *Wonders of the Seven Seas*, or something similar, and its pages were littered with the weird and the wonderful, including the devastatingly unknown inky blackness of deep sea and the occasional toothy grin of a shark.

Sharks were the thing of adolescent boy dreams. James Bond wrestled 'em; their fins cut menacingly around cinematic doomed shipmates; their skins were like sandpaper and they never grew ill. I remember pictures from this book clearly, thirty-five years later – one was of a blue shark taking a mouthful out of an unfortunate – and I hoped already dead – bottle-nose dolphin.

I can still feel the sense of gross compulsion as I stared into the pages at the off-pink ragged tissue that surrounded the shark's bite. It wasn't like my flesh, I pondered – more rubbery and stringy, a different colour and possessed of an other-worldliness. This image, combined with the darkness of the night sea around it, coloured both my dreams and my early forays into story writing for years to come.

There was another further on in this book, too. The first few I could flick through and study at leisure, for they were photos of the mighty great white, and scary as he was, he was fascinating too.

The next pic was of a great white attack victim. The image was small and grainy, but in contrast to the pictures of the bottle-nose dolphin's mutilated flesh, this was human in the extreme – disturbingly red and raw. It was the flesh of a man called Rodney Fox – or should I say what was left of the flesh of a man called Rodney Fox – lying on a hospital bed. He looked like the leftovers from a butcher's block.

In December 1963, Mr Fox had been spearfishing thirty-one miles south of Adelaide. He was a champion spear-fisherman and had spent his lifetime in and around the ocean off southern Australia.

During a competition to defend his title, his luck ran out. He bumped into a hungry great white shark and they didn't tip their trilbies, say, 'Pardon me', and carry on their merry

ways. Fox was comprehensively munched. The attack is still regarded as one of the most miraculous in all shark-attack history – because Rodney Fox survived.

He was dragged from the waves and rushed to hospital, despite his friends thinking he was done for. His abdomen was exposed and his lung torn. His spleen was revealed. An artery was gashed, so blood loss was huge. His right hand and arm were thought beyond saving. Incredibly, doctors battled to save him and kept him, minus some truly monumental scars – in one piece. During surgery to piece him back together, he needed 462 stitches. These were the pictures I saw in that book.

As I grew older, I, of course, was baited into watching *Jaws* by my two older brothers. The scene from that Spielberg classic that sticks with me is the bloody stump of a severed leg dropping to the bottom of the ocean trailing blood.

So, my formative years built the great white along the same lines in my subconscious as the Tyrannosaurus Rex – and the great white was by no means extinct.

The fascination never really left me, I realise now. When I was a teenager and living in my first shared house, I infuriated my other housemates – one of whom was Wal, by coincidence – by taking control of the TV remote during Discovery Channel 'Shark Week' and not letting anyone else near it.

And then, that fateful night down the pub. I woke up the next morning with a hangover. Nothing unusual there. But what was unusual was the seed that had been planted. I wanted to exorcise the demon. I wanted to see the real thing.

I was unmarried, in a decent job and without heavy financial responsibilities. I began saving.

And so it is, several months later, still somewhat bemused as to how it had all come to pass, Wal and I find ourselves in Gansbaai, South Africa, the great white shark diving capital of the world. It's on the southern-most tip of the African continent, a stretch east around the coastline from the Cape of Good Hope.

Here, the chilly waters of the Atlantic crash ferociously into the heel of the African continent, bringing rich seams of aquatic life – from tiny krill to feed the whales to pinnipeds to feed the earth's mightiest predator.

Gansbaai is yet another one-horse town. Rambling low blocks of hardware stores and bars lead, eventually, to the sea. There's nowhere else to go. And every bar, every sign, every shopfront, every café and everybody has some sort of link to the great white sharks that cruise, torpedo like, off Gansbaai's shores.

'Welcome,' cries the large lady with a karate chop of an Afrikaans accent.

'Welcome to the world of the great white shark.'

It's actually the world of a whitewashed bungalow a short drive from the spit of land that forms Gansbaai's thriving metropolis of shark action, but the walls are plastered with photos of fearsome-looking teeth and red raw gums. And they were just the shark wranglers.

> **And every bar, every sign, every shopfront, every café and everybody has some sort of link to the great white sharks that cruise, torpedo like, off Gansbaai's shores.**

Every other house along this street seems to have been converted into a shark diving operation. It's obviously big business and – as with any other – there appears to be a fair degree of separation between both the budget and deluxe opportunities to get up close and personal with *Carcharodon carcharias*.

We've chosen something akin to middle-of-the-road, budget-wise. I hope that means our cage stays afloat.

You've probably seen variations of cage diving many times on your TV screens. Beloved of wildlife documentary makers, these open panelled mesh frames are suspended in the upper surface of the water, affording the wetsuit-wearing denizens within a bird's eye view of the underwater realm of the shark without having to risk life or limb.

Their use is controversial, though.

Accepted practice when trying to attract sharks is to ladle stinking buckets of blood and fish guts – chum – into the ocean, leaving a snaking slick of oily attractors that are supposed to funnel passing sharks in the direction of the cage.

We've been told repeatedly in those 'Shark Week' shows that sharks can pick up tiny levels of blood in large amounts of water, thanks to the array of senses arranged along their sensitive snouts. So these snail trails of surface gunk should sound an underwater klaxon to the passing great white.

Abalone divers in South Australia believe chumming has changed the behaviour of great whites over the years, reducing their natural caution of man (hah!) and making them more inclined to hang around and investigate boats. Cage dive operators naturally refute this, saying they're just making the most of the shark's natural behaviour.

Wal and I are encouraged to take a seat in the waiting room while we wait for other guests. A small TV is playing loops of spectacular shark footage in one corner. There are slow motion replays of clashing, extendable jaws pounding great hunks of tuna fish into nothing but frayed rope. The little knot in my stomach tightens a tad more.

Just then through the open doors comes the sound of squealing brakes, raised voices, yells in the street. The large lady takes a laconic look outside and then comments to no one in particular, 'Pick-up's just ran over that guy's Jack Russell. He's not happy.'

Then she claps her hands and gives us a full-beam grin.

'Right! Let's get this show on the road. Who wants to dive with great white sharks?'

The boat is a regular affair, with a spotting deck higher up, and the handful of us due to sail that day are given a few brief instructions. As non-divers, we couldn't wear scuba gear. We'd have to make do with wetsuits and face masks and simply take a deep breath before submerging when a leviathan dutifully appeared. We would power out to an area a mile or so offshore, bait it and begin the waiting game. It could take all day, we were warned. There was no guarantee we'd see anything – and no guarantee of a refund if we didn't. Wal and I exchange a look. It's a bloody long way from the pub to spend the day bobbing about on the briny blue.

The boat is a regular affair, with a spotting deck higher up, and the handful of us due to sail that day are given a few brief instructions.

If a passing shark was spotted, however, our wrangler would immediately throw out a lure – a big piece of fish tied onto a line – and try and bring the beast close to the boat by dragging it in front of him, just out of reach. At this stage, some of us would be told to get in the cage quick. And get ready to take a deep breath and dunk.

As we charge out of Gansbaai harbour, green surf spraying into the wind, sheepish grins are exchanged. I wonder if Wal feels like I did: a little cold despite the warm sun. My overpowering thought is, 'Will I have the bottle to do it when the time comes?' There is no way of telling without putting myself to the test.

After a crafty bit of negotiation with the skipper (Wal's a master at this sort of thing) we are advised to get our wetsuits on as we'll be the first cabs off the rank if the opportunity arises. I'm not sure if I am pleased about this as I set about squeezing myself into a suit. But Wal shows no sign of backing out, so I don't really feel I can. After all, it was my bloody silly idea.

Then, a mile or so out into the ocean, we start 'chumming' – tossing out the fish soup goodies to bring the predators a-prowlin'.

Not a lot happens. The sun pours down from an unbroken sky and yet the sea breeze ensures we keep our fleeces to hand. We chat intermittently, not really listening. And as the boat bucks and dips in the feisty waters, we also keep a lookout. I find myself staring into the murky depths around the boat, trying to square away the fact that just feet away there may be man-eating monsters circling us. When we climb up to the spotting deck in order to defeat the glare of the sun on the water, I cling with exaggerated intensity as I tiptoe around the rail-thin side of the cabin and grab for the ladder.

And as the boat bucks and dips in the feisty waters, we also keep a lookout.

One slip, I tell myself, might be all it would take; you don't want to be falling in there. It's not as if the ocean is packed to the rafters with sharks I'm sure, but I feel hunted just the same. Coming from a country where the most dangerous animal is a deer coming through your windscreen means I'm not used to the boot being on the other foot; I'm not used to things that want to tear and render my delicate flesh. Apart from my dear wife, of course. And let's face it, at the British seaside all you have to worry about is the weather, broken glass and the occasional part-buried dog turd.

About two hours in, standing atop the boat, I see an unmistakable shadow cruising towards the stern.

'Shark!' I yell squeakily and point. And the race is on.

It so happens that I choose this time to get started on an uncontrollable fit of the giggles. I sometimes do, often in the most unfortunate of circumstances. I once nearly brought a Remembrance Day orchestral concert to a halt with my series of snorts, squeaks, shudders and gulps. Shameful, I know, but once past a certain point, I just can't help myself. A sort of hysteria sets in.

'Shut up, you idiot,' mutters Wal as we don our masks and make our way to the side of the boat, the rest of the crowd watching, where the cage is already thrashing about alarmingly in the maelstrom of the increasingly stroppy seas.

Ah, the cage. It looks like a considered assault from a battery hen would render it useless. Instead of the vast iron planks I had envisaged cowering behind, it consists of nothing more than bars no thicker than my little finger. It is cylindrical in shape, around ten feet deep with a vast, gaping hole in the top. It stays afloat thanks to dodgy-looking empty liquid containers lashed haphazardly to the top and sides.

I eye it dubiously again. This is not a great idea. I giggle some more.

We are shooed in by the skipper. I'd been expecting a millpond-calm viewing experience, but this is nothing of the sort. The boat wallows and churns amid the swells, the cage rising and falling alarmingly and crashing against the boat only to spring away a couple of feet with the arrival of the next wave.

What if I fall in between it and the boat?

I don't have time to reconsider. I am on the side of the boat, legs over the edge and suddenly into the mouth of the cage – and not that of a shark, thankfully. The water is cold despite the wetsuit and I discover that giggling invited cold seawater into my lungs, so I even stop that for a short while.

I don't have time to reconsider. I am on the side of the boat, legs over the edge and suddenly into the mouth of the cage – and not that of a shark, thankfully.

Down I go; the world turns silent and turquoise in an instant. I reach for the side of the cage to try and hold position. But as it dances and sways, so do my arms and legs, haphazardly poking out between the bars as I desperately try to stay within its confines. What if our toothy friend passes by while I am waving my appendages appealingly at him through the bars of the cage? It'll be like offering a kebab to a salivating pit bull.

Wal is suddenly in beside me and we rise to the surface, clinging on to the cage and each other for dear life, gasping, spluttering, giggling (me).

'What the **** are we doing here?!' Wal says, somewhat crossly, as we are tossed around the cage like shirts in a washing machine.

'What have you got me into now?' he continues, his face as white as a sheet. I supposed mine was too, but I couldn't tell, so I giggle and swallow seawater instead.

From sea level, we can't see much apart from the rising side of the boat, but now we are in it's a case of waiting for a signal from the skipper that a fish is somewhere nearby. Until then, we have time to kill.

Forty-five minutes we tread water in that cage. Until our teeth chatter and our lips turn blue. We don't say a lot to each other. We wait and watch seagulls wheel overhead and try to keep our arms and legs out of harm's way.

Forty-five minutes is a long time to ponder a potentially horrible death. Admittedly, my research has revealed that no one has ever been eaten while studying great whites in a cage. But wouldn't it be just my luck to break the duck?

'SHARK!' comes the cry, loud and clear and then suddenly comes the twitching rope, spinning droplets of water past the cage as the skipper pulls it in past us as fast as his arms can work. I take a deep breath and plunge.

Again, eerie silence. Motes of plankton and sea debris dance in front of my vision. Bubbles and foam splash overhead. And an image I'll never forget.

Straight past the cage, like a 737 lifting in take-off, soars the shockingly white underbelly of a great white shark. Unmistakable in silhouette, the shark's pectoral fins cleave water and block out sun.

Apparently, it wasn't that massive – ten feet or so in length, we were later told. But it looks vast and as it glides over it appears to mince the rope bait in slow motion, great serrated teeth reaching, chomping, reaching, chomping. Flecks of ragged tuna flesh and soft pink gouts of seawatery blood puff from the shark's extended gills as it passes.

And then it is gone. Prehistoric. Monumental. Magnificent.

And then it is gone. Prehistoric. Monumental. Magnificent.

I feel a scrabbling pressure, a hand on my shoulder and then, unmistakably, a foot on my head. I am shoved to the bottom of the cage.

My head is still reeling at the sight of the shark and my compass is scrambled. I try to lift to the top of the cage and merely bang my head on the bottom. I right myself and try again.

I bang the cage once more. Odd. I'm confused. Sure I'm the right way up, I begin to carefully ascend to the top of the cage only to find a commotion and instant demotion once I get there, something shoving me hard back into the depths. All this excitement on one breath of air. I really must think about taking another. Really quite soon.

I'm sure this strange episode lasted but seconds, but in the time lapse of my memory, it happens over and over again in ultra-slow motion. I wonder ponderously if I am to dodge death by shark and drown in a shark cage instead.

Suddenly, the threshing above subsides, and with sunlight pouring back down from above, I get my bearings and rise, gasping, to the surface. I look up to the boat. Wal is peering over the side, looking rather sheepish.

'Sorry boy,' he says.

It appears my dear friend had decided enough was enough at the entrance of the shark, and had opted to leave the cage early in an orderly manner. Except that he forgot the orderly part.

Wal came face to face with the fight or flight syndrome – and flight won. He scrambled hard for purchase against the thin bars and whenever he came into contact with me, he used me as a human stepladder. Each time he toppled back in as the waves bumped him off his precarious perch, he started from the bottom rung again, using my noggin as a handily placed stirrup.

Bastard.

I'm hauled onto the familiar surface of the boat and lie gasping, giggling, still spouting seawater. The other seagoers gather around, asking questions – had we seen it, was it big, was it scary, was it still there?

I look across at Wal and offer a weary high five. We burst out laughing.

There is a massive adrenaline rush that lasts for ages afterwards. We stand in our wetsuits, the hot African sun warming our chilled bones, grinning like kids, arms around shoulders.

What would you do if you had no fear? Dive with great white sharks, of course. And we had. There's some satisfaction to be had in that, you know.

The rest of the boat trip is a hazy memory. We had no desire to go back into the depths – we'd had our turn. We sat in the stern, top halves of our wetsuits peeled down, salt drying on our skins. I reached for my backpack and pulled out what was to me – and the rest of the world, for that matter – a new cigar.

The man behind it was destined for bigger and better things in the cigar world, but he didn't know it just yet. The Cuban ex-pat had but a tiny shop in Miami's Little Havana, with a dozen rollers turning out some ravingly good Nicaraguan cigars. The man was Don Pepin García and my smoke on the water was the Cuban Classic Black Label in robusto size.

With a trembling hand, I lit up the cigar and looked out across the vast, deadly, fascinating, ocean. We sat all afternoon in the back of that boat. I shall remember those hours all of my days.

The Cuban ex-pat had but a tiny shop in Miami's Little Havana, with a dozen rollers turning out some ravingly good Nicaraguan cigars.

It wasn't until we'd finally made it back to our HQ at Hermanus later that night, (incidentally, the whale-watching capital of the world – you can see them from the clifftops in season) and prepared ourselves for a celebratory meal that I realised I'd burned my face to a crisp without realising it. Ah well. Looking like a lobster while eating one was a price I was more than willing to pay.

CHAPTER NINE

Rainforest

THE DESERT WAS BAD, BUT NOTHING COULD COMPARE WITH
THE HORRORS OF A TROPICAL RAIN FOREST.

— *Tahir Shah,* In Search of King Solomon's Mines

Finding a red-eyed, hairy, dripping-wet pig – so big that its back is higher than my belt buckle – standing in your path on your way back to bed isn't an everyday occurrence, you'd have to agree.

Then again, on consideration, if you live in the rainforest in Borneo, perhaps it jolly well is.

The beast grunts at us happily enough and resumes its wet squelching through the rainforest floor. Which, incidentally, may as well be the riverbed, as it's under-water and invisible to the eye.

It has rained since my wife and I arrived this morning. And when I say rain, I'm not really sure I'm doing the term justice. This is rain Noah would have recognised. Sheets of torrential water cascading from a near-dark sky; thunder and lightning louder and more fantastic than any I've ever heard or seen since. In these climes – in the middle of bloody nowhere, if I'm honest – it's oppressively warm at all hours of the day or night, so you walk around as if with a dustbin-lid-sized super showerhead suspended above you with

The beast grunts at us happily enough and resumes its wet squelching through the rainforest floor.

the handle stuck in the full-on, water-to-hot position.

This trip had seemed such a good idea while tucked up in our massive luxury hotel in Kota Kinabalu. There, the only decision of the day to make was which of the pools should we lounge by, or which of the fancy restaurants should we dine in that evening.

I swear choruses of angels rang through the air when I walked into the vast lobby of the Sutera Harbour, and after first being wowed by the great view of the South China Sea, was then floored by the sight of a cigar lounge – complete with bar and walk-in humidor – right there off to one side of the lobby. Holy moly. I was going to enjoy this place.

And so I had, with evenings in the delightful surroundings of the lounge, drinking green tea or a glass of something stronger, playing my new wife at Connect 4 (it kept her happy) and partaking in something delightful from the humidor.

Food here was fantastic: as much seafood as you can scarf at rock-bottom prices. You could select the lobster or prawn of your choice – hell, even the prawns were a foot long – and it would be whisked away to be returned shortly with rice, a spicy sauce and a cold bottle of Tiger beer. Heaven.

But then we'd made the fatal mistake of venturing into the unknown – on the cheap.

'I would advise you to spend a little extra money and go with a more, erm, select guide,' said an affable British chap who ran a local tourist service and who had dropped in to chat to new arrivals and offer his expertise on the attractions and excursions.

We were young, we were foolish, we knew better.

We smiled politely, nodded, thanked him and booked onto a well-known budget-camp provider instead.

After a seemingly endless bumping, grinding bus journey, we pile into narrowboats and power up the wide expanse of the Kinabatangan river, the wake from our prow curling away and splashing up the muddy banks fifty metres away. We are on our way into the rainforest. Orangutans and all that.

It is blazingly hot. The sort of heat that drips and sucks and pulls the energy from you. I put my lunchtime queasiness and sleepiness down to this alone, mop my feverish brow and keep quiet.

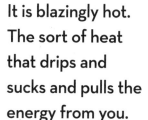

It is blazingly hot. The sort of heat that drips and sucks and pulls the energy from you.

Hour after hour passes with the high drone of the boat engine and the unending sweep of the river. The undergrowth on the banks grows deeper, greener, taller. Soon exotic birds flap ostentatiously in front of us. We have left civilisation behind.

Earlier that morning, I had developed a dull, nagging pain in my lower right belly. And rather than face it, I'd pretended it wasn't there. But it was. And as each mile passed, as another hour ticked by, it was gnawing at my insides.

Once it reached a screeching crescendo, I knew what it was. But it was too late to do anything about it, so I slump in the bottom of the boat and pretend to go to sleep.

What a time for your appendix to play up.

Since my teens I'd suffered from a queer pain that everyone laughed off as a 'grumbling appendix'. It was no laughing matter to me. A needling, eventually white-hot pain would rise in a point to the right of my lower belly and reach enough of a crescendo to be debilitating, occasionally accompanied by bouts of acute nausea and disorientation. Once, I was hospitalised for five days while they tried to figure out what was wrong. In the end, the pain disappeared and they kicked me out.

Ever since then – seemingly at the most inopportune moments in my life – it will suddenly flare up. I have a dread of it sneaking up on me and I had a suspicion what it was from the moment it first pin-pricked my consciousness this morning with an insidious, vindictive stab in my abdomen.

Soon, I would be hundreds of miles from the nearest town, let alone medical care. And I'd be in grave danger if the worst did occur and the blasted appendix finally burst, pouring its poison into my bloodstream.

Our boat speeds on, hour after hour, heading into seeming *Apocalypse Now* country. I slink lower in my seat; the clouds hunker down with me and darkness gathers a little closer.

It isn't long before my wife notices something is amiss.

Sotto voce, I inform her that the old appendix is playing up. Her expression is not one I'll forget in a hurry. Our hopes for a couple of days of adventure in the rainforest are taking on sinister proportions.

I wasn't kidding when I spoke of the prodigious rain a little earlier. Even by Borneoan standards, it's a deluge. We've been warned that conditions at the camp aren't as dry as they'd like.

I've seen ocean floors drier than our campsite.

When we finally pull around a bend in the river, it is just visible above lapping waves. The ear-splitting fart of the engine finally quits and we coast in to a narrow bay. A cluster of roughly timbered stand-to buildings and plank walkways is all there is of our new home.

The rest is underwater. Our boatload of similar young thrill-seekers look as if they've bitten off more thrill than they sought, too. And the little, foul-toothed ruffian 'leading' our trip jumps with a splash into the water and motions for us to join him. We dare not go in.

Was this not the land of the legendary swimming snake, whose swift bite would render you deader than a dead thing in double-quick time? Was it not the same swampy hinterland which housed a million poisonous and pissed-off spiders, which were no doubt floating about on bits of debris, desperate to sink their venomous fangs into a passing piece of soft flesh just to release a bit of pent-up frustration?

But wade in we do after a while, bare-footed and unaware exactly where we are treading, or what we are treading on.

'Ugh, this is horrendous,' my wife says, and it is. Imagine it with a hot poker embedded in your guts, I think.

The night wears on in similar fashion. To get to what is laughingly called the dining room, you have to wade. To get to what is laughingly called the toilet, you have to wade. To get to what is laughingly called your bed for the night you have to wade, bypass the devil pig along the way, climb a ladder, avoid the rats and look up through your mosquito net, wondering what giant multilegged monstrosity is likely to drop on top of it next. Dear reader, I wouldn't wish it on my worst enemy.

To add to the frisson of disappointment we feel, we have to share with a fat, hairy, obnoxious English schoolteacher who doesn't give a flying fox for our sensitivities and who drops off to sleep perchance to snore, bubblingly loud, for the next eight hours.

'How are you?' my wife asks anxiously as we place anything perishable or soft into a large metal container so that the rats won't eat it. You know, soap, toothpaste, our eyeballs, that sort of thing.

'How do I look?' I groan as we stand in our hovel, braced against the snore of the fat bastard in the next bed.

She flashes a light.

'Not good,' she eventually says, reluctantly. 'But then I don't suppose I'm at my sparkling best.'

She isn't either, all chivalry aside. The khaki shirt and shorts number were now stained and sodden, filthy and torn and the cute little flowerpot hat she'd bought at a market in town now looked more like an elephant turd after desiccation and rehydration. And so to bed.

It is my longest night on this earth.

The pain grows intense and I try not to groan or wriggle around to get more comfortable. Every time I move a muscle, my wife sits bolt upright and asks inane questions. I guess she thought each new squirm could be my last, but it was bloody tiresome.

And so, I lie on my back and watch lightning flash across the sky and hear the rain hammering on the corrugated tin roof and the scarcely-to-be-believed snores of the teacher beside us.

Oh, and the rev of a powerboat engine and the whoops and hollers of drunken young men trying to impress drunken young women. The filthy bleeder 'leading' the expedition is being fawned over by some dopy young foreigner among us and so is hooning around, showing his virility and drinking as much cheap booze as he can. As well as roaring about in the dark on the camp's only boat.

What would happen if my appendix burst? Am I about to end my days in this godforsaken hellhole of a watery grave? These, and other warming thoughts, occupy my mind until, as the grey of dawn shifts through the wooden slats and weird cries echo from the jungle, I fall into an uneasy, sweaty doze.

I awake in the morning no better, but at least no worse. And as they usually do, things seem more bearable in the cold light of morning. Until I need to avail myself of the facilities.

The camp toilet is a tin hut and hole contraption long since flooded, so the best I can do is wade somewhere in its general vicinity, away from the populace of the camp, and seek a little privacy.

And as soon as I drop my trousers, a squadron of sandfly take their opportunity to feast on human flesh. The sandfly bite is seemingly inconsequential at first, but if you're one of those unfortunate souls who react badly – like, of course, my good self – then prepare yourself for an ordeal.

By the time I've waded back to the rest of the group for our 'breakfast', such as it was, red welts have appeared up and down my legs. Within minutes these are swelling alarmingly – scores and scores of them – and an itching like none I can describe is pulsing through my lower limbs.

'I want to chop my own legs off!' I moan over hot coffee and I am only half joking. Imagine the worst mosquito bite you've ever had and multiply it by several hundred. That's what it feels like.

The sandflies are the final straw. We can't stay here a moment longer.

My wife informs the hungover buck-toothed individual in charge that we are going home that morning and asks that he prepare the boat. He is amazed and can't see what all the fuss is about. But when he comes down to the water to fire up the engine, all but one of the guests in the camp has packed and ran down to beat him to it and leap into the boat. We can't wait to escape.

And so begins the long journey home, which is infinitely better than the one there because with every passing mile we are nearer safety and further away from that hellish campsite. And, of course, the closer we get to civilisation, the less my appendix gurgles and spasms.

We reach Kota Kinabalu in a state of almost religious fervour. It is as much as I can do not to kiss the doorman of the Sutera Harbour as we step from our taxi, and I swear tears sprang to my eyes with the sight and the smell of the dear little cigar lounge. We spend the next three days ordering room service, lounging in our bath looking out to the South China Sea and accumulating suntans by the pool. We needed a top up of top-end.

My leg bites itch less but turn into weeping blisters and are a sight to behold. I have to be careful in this wet heat that infection doesn't set in. And without maligning Borneo, which is one of the most fascinating and exhilarating of all places I've visited, its culture is not the cleanest.

Sit down at a city bar or café and the old man next to you will think nothing of hawking up and expectorating – loudly and efficiently on the floor. Large, gimlet-eyed rats roamed with impunity and the stench of open sewers or rotting fish are never far away in the city.

We sheepishly seek the help of the friendly British tourist chap once more. He takes one look at us and gives a chuckle.

'Ah,' he says. 'I did warn you.'

He pushes a small box across the desk to me.

'Try one of these. They're local and actually not half bad.'

I lift the lid and nestled inside is a rough batch of torpedo cigars. I look up at him with piteous gratitude in my eyes. What a guy.

Sit down at a city bar or café and the old man next to you will think nothing of hawking up and expectorating – loudly and efficiently on the floor.

When we had sufficiently recovered from our ordeal, he sent us on a trip that will live with us for the rest of our lives. Under the kind leadership of a tribesman who led us deep into his heartland of longhouses and shrunken heads, we saw giant wasps; made incense from their huge elongated nests; spotted golden-kneed orb spiders the size of your hand; watched proboscis monkeys chat and swing among the treetops; laughed at the claw-waving mangrove crabs; ate ants; went on night hikes through the rainforest; found lichen that glowed in the dark; and marvelled at the ear-splitting, never-ending shriek of a billion cicadas.

The facilities were practical and spartan, but clean and comfortable. We travelled high in the mountains to find cold and mist and hillsides of orchids and pitcher plants and ate foot-long prawns washed dow with ice-cold Tiger beer. We snorkelled and snoozed, strolled around the wonderful city of Kuching and sniggered at those brave (or daft) enough to climb Mount Kinabalu.

And wonder of wonders, on one of our last magical nights, when moonlight spread slowly across the gently lapping ocean and lianas draped and veiled our romantic walk down to a little jungle hut where we were invited to grab a beer and a humble cooked meal, I was gobsmacked to find a television. A flickering, snow-screened, but nonetheless working, television in the middle of a rainforest island.

A flickering, snow-screened, but nonetheless working, television in the middle of a rainforest island.

And we laughed at the preposterousness of it all when we realised the guides, locals, pigs and goats had gathered to watch my beloved Manchester United. It was the moment to pull out a long-tubed cigar from my pack.

I suspected the humidity here meant I'd have a constant re-light on my hands, but it seemed the perfect moment. So, I dusted off an Illusione I'd been saving for a special occasion. It couldn't get a more surreal and therefore perfect moment to salute Dion Giolito, creator of Illusione, and a lovely guy to boot.

Dion loves out-of-the-box thinking and the quirkier side of life. This little scene would appeal to him no end, I thought. And so, to admiring glances from friendly residents, I puffed the stick and watched United.

By the end of the night, we were passing the remains of my cigar around for communal tasting, and we drank Tiger beer long into the pitch black, cicada-screaming, jungle-deadly night.

CHAPTER TEN

Up, Up and Away

Clouds come into my life, no longer to carry rain or usher storm, but to add colour to my sunset sky.

— Rabindranath Tagore

I've never quite made it to the stage of enjoying a hand-rolled cigar while reclining in the comfy seat of a private jet – yet. I'm saving that one for *Around The World in 80 Cigars – Again.*

But in the meantime, I have had another aerial adventure worthy of recall.

Baptiste Loiseau is a young man on a mission. Taking the reins from Rémy Martin's renowned cellar master, Pierrette Trichet, is not a job for the faint-hearted. She's something of a legend in the trade, the first lady to hold the position across any of France's major Cognac houses and the creator and curator of many a fine example of the *eau de vix* that lie, dormant but not dead, in the dusty cellars spread across this peaceful landscape of chalk and cheese.

Whitewashed *maisons* in the village of Saint-Preuil lie somnabulant in the midday sun. Swifts dip and scream among the beams of old barns. Roadside poppies flourish.

Swifts dip and scream among the beams of old barns. Roadside poppies flourish.

I love France. Its insolence, occasional indolence, its indifference to passing of time and stubborn adherence to the things that matter. Like food, farming, wine and loved ones. The Frenchman assumes a God-given right, nay duty, to stop regularly at sociable local cafés for regular top-ups of strong, inky-black coffee; he indulges in pungent cheese and crusty white bread without bothering to dignify the clamour from health scaremongers. He'll reach for a smoke if he wants one; and his food is treated with reverence, or rather *love*.

> He'll reach for a smoke if he wants one; and his food is treated with reverence, or rather *love.*

One day I should like to buy a little cottage somewhere rural and quiet in France – with a suitable market town nearby, of course – and have the time to settle into some of its seasonal rhythms. I've always secretly hankered after a crumbly old place, with great wooden shutters on the windows where I could park myself around the back in the shade of a walnut tree and doze through the afternoon drone of ring-necked doves and the buzz of the bees in the orchard.

I've been lucky enough to smoke long, elegant lancero-sized cigars while sliding down the Loire in a sailboat; enjoy a floral Rafael González with a glass of fizz and a bowl of clams collected from a D-Day beach in Normandy.

I've tasted 1918 Armagnac and a glorious Dominican La Aurora in the land of ducks and geese deep in southern France, and shared many a good cigar and many more laughs with my friend the French cigar explorer, Guillaume Tesson. But the day I sipped on a Davidoff Churchill as I glided serenely over the vineyards of Cognac was a good one.

It is still twilight when I emerge sleepily from the hotel in the market square of Jarnac. The lights in the *boucherie* across the road aren't even on. Typically, it has been another late night of gentle carousing and it would be fair to say that I am perhaps not on my most sparkling of form in the chilly pre-dawn breeze. I've never been one of those morning people. You know the ones I mean: they are able, when the alarm clock clears its throat, to leap out of bed with a gay tra-la-la on their lips.

My wife is one. She is up, nattering, banging cupboards, opening curtains, switching on lights, turning on radios and generally behaving like a She Devil before sensible souls have fully come around.

I would refute allegations of grumpiness. Left to my own devices and not pestered with questions about mortgages, travel arrangements, dog-walking timetables or school-hockey fixtures; left with time to put on the kettle, perform silent ablutions, marshal one's thoughts for the day and generally ease oneself into the upright once more, I am fine and dandy.

It's just that I'm not often, in a household of three girls, a dog and two hamsters, often afforded such good manners. So don't be surprised if, when you call me early doors to discuss the latest developments in luxury Knightsbridge knitwear, if you receive a less than enthusiastic response. You've been warned.

This morning I am, thankfully, only required to harrumph at my morning wake-up call from the receptionist and stumble outside. The Charente twinkles merrily under the glow of an occasional streetlight as my driver pulls away from the village and through the gloaming streets. I doze a little, uncomfortably propped between cold glass and the

It's just that I'm not often, in a household of three girls, a dog and two hamsters, often afforded such good manners.

headrest, until we stop to ask directions in gruff French and bump our way eventually across a sloping field to where a hot air balloon – or, more magnificently, *montgolfière*, as the French would poetically call it – is billowing amid the dew.

With sharp, dragon-breath bursts of flame from the basket-mounted canister lying on its side, the huge canopy is filling. Within twenty minutes – during which I am thankful for a proffered flask of hot coffee and a few thin biscuits – the basket is upright, I am in it, and with the pilot firmly in charge, am lifting, gently but purposefully, from terra firma.

'*À bientôt!*' comes the cry from the roadcrew below and then silence falls across an awakening countryside. We rise towards trees on a seemingly inescapable collision course, but at the last moment, the basket merely scratches the uppermost branches and then we are soaring, unencumbered, into the brightening morning sky. My hangover lifts and clears with the bottom of the basket. I am awake.

A sparrowhawk scuds along the hedgerow below, seemingly oblivious to the shadow passing above. Cattle graze in geometric shapes. Snail-paced cars edge down worm-thin lanes. Great estates become mere play parks; lakes filled with skulking, slimy tench become puddles in the green desert.

I'm not a massive fan of heights – I have no desire to fling myself from a perfectly serviceable aeroplane in a skydive, for example – but travelling in a *montgolfière* holds no sense of fear of falling – for me, at least. Just a sense of wonder and delight at this unique perspective of everyday objects. The only noise is from the occasional blast of the furnace that feeds hot air into the canvas above us.

> **A sparrowhawk scuds along the hedgerow below, seemingly oblivious to the shadow passing above.**

Dogs inevitably rush barking into farmyards, no doubt awakening sleepy, ill-tempered farmers. Early rising washerwomen stare up from their clotheslines. And apart from the demonic blasts aforementioned, which at least keep the top of your head toasty, the silence is emancipating. It's not often you get to travel with vistas such as these on the horizon without the accompanying fanfare of engine noise.

It's a glorious rural French morning. Row after carefully tended row of vines snake across the valley. Now a solitary kestrel hangs, as if suspended by a single piano wire, in between rows, eyes intent on a lizard or rodent below. Sun warms my face, as does, in true hedonistic style, a wee splash of Rémy. It feels staggeringly louche to drink Cognac for breakfast, but I'm sure it's not the first time it's happened in the French countryside.

And so, as firsts are being ticked off personal lists, I dig in my pocket for the Davidoff Churchill I've secreted there for just such an occasion. I've never smoked a cigar in a hot-air balloon before. And, Dear Reader, I still haven't because I'm told it's bloody dangerous and could have resulted in various parts of me showering the French countryside in gore while a burning basket plummeted to earth. So instead, I must wait a while.

And so, as firsts are being ticked off personal lists, I dig in my pocket for the Davidoff Churchill I've secreted there for just such an occasion.

We drift across the countryside for an hour or so, spying pin-steepled churches in little market towns. I'd forgotten sleepy country communities like this still exist.

And when we eventually land with a soft bump in the headland of a grass field, it's with a sense of exhilaration coupled with an extraordinary serenity. Of course, with that magnificent debauchment the French seem to manage so effortlessly, we're welcomed back down to earth with a glass of something *to settle the stomach*. Of course, given the present company, it's a glass of Cognac. And I take the opportunity to settle it with something from the tobacco fields of Cuba.

We drift across the countryside for an hour or so, spying pin-steepled churches in little market towns. I'd forgotten sleepy country communities like this still exist.

The cigar is perhaps a little robust for this time in the morning (as is the Cognac, if we're being honest), but this is something which just had to be done. How many opportunities for a balloon basket breakfast are you going to have in your life? So, my cigar is fired up and I sip breakfast Cognac. Oh là là!

Taking a trip in a *montgolfière* is Zen in the extreme; a lesson in mindfulness. It's helped, of course, by the straight, true burn of the cigar and its flavour, which punctuates, not penetrates, my reverie over the beautiful French countryside this morning.

Did I mention, I do love France?

CHAPTER ELEVEN

Henke

'LIKE CROSSING NIAGARA ON A BICYCLE'; IT'S AN EXPRESSION
IN THE DOMINICAN REPUBLIC THAT BASICALLY SAYS
SOMEONE IS GOING THROUGH A HARD TIME.

— *Juan Luis Guerra*

If you've ever met one of your heroes, you'll realise it's a bit like being a schoolkid in front of the headmaster all over again.

That excruciating mix of excitement, trepidation, anxiety to please, and, as you already know, in my case an overwhelming urge to giggle, which can be off-putting to headmasters and heroes alike.

On this occasion, I've travelled all the way to Dominican Republic and it's a hero, not a headmaster, I'm walking up a muddy field to meet. It's pre-dawn in cigar country.

Cigar plantations are spectacularly beautiful. Row upon row of thick green foliage shines from the well-tilled soil below. Often shielded by distant hillsides, nestled in hollows and valleys and bathed by the sun for most of the day, they are mesmerising places to be.

But as the sun rises for the first time over the horizon and a new day dawns, there's an excitement in the pit of my stomach that isn't there just because it's time to break my overnight fast.

> **Cigar plantations are spectacularly beautiful. Row upon row of thick green foliage shines from the well-tilled soil below.**

My taxi stops aside a gateway into greenness and I'm beginning the walk up the sticky track when the unmistakeable figure of Henke Kelner comes around the corner. I once described Henke as the Steven Spielberg of the cigar world, and I reckon that's still a pretty good way to begin my description here.

Think of some of the best New World cigars you've tasted and there's every chance that somewhere along the line, Henke's had his hand in it.

He ran the Tabadom facility, which became the new producer for Davidoff cigars in the 1990s. And since then, his unparalleled skill with tobacco has seen scores of lines, blends trials and techniques become mainstream.

Which is why, when I reach to shake Henke's hand in that field of tobacco near Santiago de Los Caballeros, as the first light of dawn sifts through his Panama hat, I'm a little lost for words.

His eyes scan me, then return to my face, birdlike curiosity playing across his features.

'We meet before, no?' he asks in his broken, though perfectly understandable, English.

'Yes!' I gush. 'We met at the Davidoff store in London at the launch of the Churchill line, we talked about seeds and flavour profiles.'

He looks on, unblinking.

'We went through the palate profile for the various sizes…' I try again.

He raises his gaze to the horizon.

'We talked about moonshine in Kentucky!'

His head swivels back to me, his craggy face breaking into a toothy grin.

'Moo'shine. Yes, Kentucky moo'shine!'

And he laughs a deep belly laugh and claps a burly hand around my shoulder, turning me up the path towards the lean-to, palm-roofed hut that awaits us.

He remembers the moonshine because we were talking about spirits of all sorts back in Mayfair, London. He told me of some of his whirlwind tours of Europe and of the US, how he loves Scotch whisky, how he discovered – and, of course, sampled – moonshine in Kentucky.

With this memory firmly back in his mind, he leads me off into the leaves and begins a morning's tobacco instruction which is as masterful and enthralling as any favourite professorial thesis.

His mind leaps from subject to subject, loosely based around cigar tobacco and its infinite variations, although by no means constrained by it.

And I follow in his wake, happy to be in his presence and soak up a little of the lifetime of knowledge he is dispensing.

At the hut, welcome now as the early morning sun begins to warm, there is a small group of staff busy concocting something. Henke leads me to them.

Some are busy boiling pots of water on stoves; others are grating large, hard-pressed lumps of cacao into fine, sweet-smelling powder.

'I grow this – and coffee – up there on my farm,' growls Henke, pointing to the distant hillsides, where coffee and cacao grow high up the slopes.

'My wife's farm.' He corrects himself with a grin and a wink.

'They never used to grow tobacco here, but I thought it could be done. I was right,' he says proudly, passing me a little porcelain espresso cup mixture of the hot water and cacao with a pinch of cinnamon.

My God in heaven, I swear I'll never forget the taste of that tiny cup as the leaves of *Nicotiana tobacum* swayed and brushed with a leathery swish against one another.

Henke leans over to a large wooden humidor and picks out two Davidoff No.2 cigars, passing me one and clipping and lighting his in one fluid motion.

I drain my cup and another follows and as I puff on the light sweet cigar and chat to Henke, the starstruck numbness drifts away. We talk of blends and varietals, of cigars he likes and those he doesn't; of Cuba and comparisons to it; of the future and of the past.

When we have had our fill of the wonderful hot chocolate and a bite or two from some pastries, we don our hats and wander back out into the sun, where workers are checking on the plants, removing withered leaves, hoeing drainage furrows up against each row.

> **My God in heaven, I swear I'll never forget the taste of that tiny cup as the leaves of *Nicotiana tobacum* swayed and brushed with a leathery swish against one another.**

And all the time, there is a constant stream of cigar talk – 99 per cent of it from Henke. Did I mention he can talk a bit?

Never mind, what he says is worth hearing, so I am content to traipse along in the shade of his big form, listening and interjecting only when I am unsure of quite what he means.

He always has a word, a backslap and a handshake for a passing worker. His critical eye seems to take in every damned leaf in that vast sea of green. And a smile is never far from his lips. I bet he was a rascal as a young 'un.

And all this was before I'd seen him dance the merengue, which I can report, he also does with aplomb. Multitalented chap is Henke.

CHAPTER TWELVE

The Great Outdoors

THE RICHNESS I ACHIEVE COMES FROM NATURE, THE SOURCE
OF MY INSPIRATION.

— *Claude Monet*

The countryside is where I love to be. I've always been a country bumpkin at heart.

I've lived in it most of my life, minus a stay or two in Sheffield and regular commutes to see the missus when she was at university in Nottingham.

Becoming intricately involved in rural life was, for me, only natural. I had an early interest in birds and beasts and my father took me down to the Grand Union Canal to catch my first fish, a glowering, red and spiny-backed, tiger-striped perch that looked huge and made my heart thump.

I got into shooting too, spending my weekends arising at some ungodly hour to tiptoe through the house and out into the wonder of the wild beyond, armed with an old air rifle and an awful lot of patience.

I look back on that time with a sense of wonder and gratitude; for it was a great introduction and a way to learn about the laws of the natural world by osmosis. The changing of the seasons were obvious in the grass underfoot and the canopy above. Birds quickly became my fascination and I soon learned all those in my vicinity: their flight, call, nesting habits, feeding places.

Inevitably, as I grew older, other influences came to the fore in my life and being outdoors alone in the countryside didn't happen as often as it used to. I missed it.

When, as an adult, I realised that I still hankered for the lonely places of the world occasionally, I fell back into my rural idyll. The occasional day's fly fishing; beating, picking up and occasionally shooting on the village shoot; working the dog on other small, informal game shoots; and getting out by myself occasionally with gun underarm once again.

I'm not a particularly religious person, but the closest I get to it is when I'm in the great outdoors in the silence: hearing the breeze in the treetops, watching a sparrowhawk work a hedge, being fortunate to catch a glimpse of a sunbathing fox. There is a pervading sense of awe of the Almighty. The countryside is my church.

And, of course, I found a new way to punctuate this re-found love of the wild: with the occasional good cigar.

Smoking outdoors is a totally different proposition. I discovered after much trial and error that the sort of stick I wanted must be relatively short and relatively fat to withstand the wind and the occasional slice of rough treatment. It must burn exceedingly well; and be lightish in flavour, nothing too powerful, but perhaps something rich and contemplative.

> ## Smoking outdoors is a totally different proposition.

I've been invited to shoot on a swathe of land not a million miles from where I live. It's a beautiful low-lying slice of England, thatched with mature beech and oak, carpeted by patchworks of oilseed rape and of barley, old hedgerows and duck-filled splashes. Grey partridge still have a foothold here, and hares lollop across stubble.

There's a sizeable wood here too, packed with deer, owls, jays, badgers and woodcock. I am very much attached to it and have worked the dog through it for many years.

Once each year, I'm invited to shoot it myself towards the end of the season – a great privilege, for although the bag is never large, it's one of the finer shoots I've been on.

One particular morning brought more than the usual shoot-day frisson of excitement when I whisked back the curtains in the growing light. Snow-flakes stuttered and stumbled earthwards from a leaden sky.

I have a childish love of snow and the blanketed, ear-ringing silence that descends on the countryside when a sizeable dollop of it drops – although that happens a lot less these days than it did in the days of my gilded youth. A snowy day then tended to mean a day off school and I remember clearly being snowed in on a number of occasions.

Heavy-duty clothing was called for today – thermals aplenty, multiple socks and gloves and – whisper it – ladies tights too. An old brick-laying pal of mine told me of this old trick on the coldest of winter days. They really do keep your hairy old legs warm. So I tried it out and he was right. You may not look the full ticket, but your nether regions will be as warm as toast. Just don't tell anyone I do this, okay?

The dog had an extra large breakfast. And we are off, loaded with cartridges, flask, lead, whistle and all the other accoutrements that seem to have become so necessary for a day in the field.

The gathering for the morning bacon butty and mug of tea is more raucous than usual, excitement palpable in the air along with our steaming breaths. And around 9 a.m. we are packed into the shoot trailer (a sheep transporter, really, filled with bales) and very soon waddling through a thin layer of snow to the first peg.

I shoot well for once; rocketing pheasants looking like hatching mayfly as they power their way overhead, long tails snaking.

Lunch comes with pork pie and hot soup in a dusty old barn. My cheeks feel like hot coals as I sit in a corner on an old rafter, brushing off casted barn owl pellets before sitting down.

Motes of snow sift through the gauze window high up on one wattle wall, increasingly heavily as we luncheoned. And by the time we step back out, a little thawed, it is snowing proper.

Thick, heavy flakes settle onto everything, including eyelashes, as I trudge across solid plough to my peg. I lay my cartridge bag and gunslip down carefully and when I look back a few minutes later could barely see them, such was the fury of the snowfall.

Just one bird comes my way – or at least one that I could actually see – another cock pheasant, dark and gold and red against the snow-flooded sky. He calls in a ringing manner as he flies fast and angular to my left at some distance, and I throw the barrels at him instinctively, forgetting technique and just swinging through.

Not thinking about it always makes me shoot better and the old bird folds in mid-air and hits the snow with an audible crump. The dog is away after him with a flurry of flakes, pouncing and skidding, his black face a now a patchwork mask.

And I stand in that maelstrom – it gets steadily worse until we are forced to call the whole thing off shortly afterwards for fear of losing guns and beaters alike – and I reached for a cigar.

It's an Alec Bradley Fine & Rare – a tiny production of ultra first-class tobacco, often developed after blenders at the company tasted something interesting in one tiny field of tobacco. It is perfect in every way.

It weathers the storm like a wave-tossed toy duck; it burns straight and true and never once do I have to relight it or touch up the edges. It is golden and captivating, compelling and nuanced, and I will never forget standing in the lee of an old oak and watching the sky fall in around me. Such priceless, timeless peace, aided and abetted by leaves carefully grown in a hot and humid foreign land.

One of the great smokes of my life.

Of course, landing a salmon in the peat-brown swirling waters of the Tweed wasn't too shabby either.

Here, below the banks of a lush grass field of highland 'coos', where midges dance and dippers bob, I dally with the mighty running salmon.

I am on assignment for dear old *Country Life* – the grand dame of British publishing, which has provided the opportunity for so many of my out-of-the-way adventures.

The folks at CL seem to have a wonderful Spidey sense when it comes to me, bless them. They seem uncannily able to tell when I have reached the end of my tether with being ensconced behind my dusty little desk in the dusty little shed at the bottom of my garden. They somehow know that the daily grind of school runs, dog walks, dinner preparations, commissions from creative agencies and boring press releases are about to finally fill my lungs and send me, kicking and spluttering, to Davy Jones' locker at the bottom of the deep and somewhat muddy pond that is the freelance writer's sanity.

And then those chirpy country types from said magazine pop up – Hasselhoff like, if you'll allow me to mangle metaphors once more – ready

to toss me a lifebuoy in the form of an intriguing and often downright odd commission to drag me back to shore.

Lobster fishing in Scotland, collecting Colchester oysters, tasting Armagnac in southern France, catching a sleeper train from London to Vienna, making charcuterie, shooting partridge, roasting suckling pig in Sardinia, lobster rolls in New England and sailing the Solent: all have come about with varying degrees of involvement of *Country Life* and its willingness to offer its readers something different. I am for ever indebted to this great old magazine.

And so here I find myself at its behest again, casting into the rushing waters in my waders, trying hard not to stumble and disappear seawards with the current.

All morning, mighty splashes have made me jump; it never fails to stagger me how such huge fish can hide undetected in such a miniscule covering of water.

Extraordinary silver-purple leviathans leap and flop back to the darkness with an almighty crash, scaring the living daylights out of me every time. Long minutes of silence are broken repeatedly in this manner, with often only a brief peripheral glimpse of the fish burning itself into my memory, gone by the time I turn my head, like a distant flash of forked lightning.

Under the expert gaze of fishing nut and Ettrick Valley Smokehouse maestro Mike Roberts, I've laboriously waded through the shallow water and positioned myself amidships. And, with a selected fly tied and waiting, I've cast and cast again in a dozen different pools.

I would have called Mike a charlatan had I not myself seen the giant ghostly leaping forms of passing salmon; without these, I would have believed the river denuded of fish.

And suddenly, just after the coos have come down to slurp and dribble and gaze dopily at the alien intruders upon their peace, I hook a salmon. At first I think it's a hooked subterranean ledge or crevice on one of the moss-covered, partly submerged stones. But when the stone begins to swim upriver, I realised something entirely different has occurred instead.

'You're on, you're on!' cries Mike excitedly, and that makes my heart pound even heavier until it feels like a medium-sized pony is giving my ribcage a jolly good kicking.

Mike leaps up onto the bank and squints down into the murk of the passing waters. 'I can see it,' he says in a matter of fact tone of voice. 'Decent fish.'

That confirmation from an expert is what does it, really. Just about sends me over the edge.

I move – fatal mistake – and nearly achieve what I've been striving to avoid all morning. Namely, disappearing upriver.

I sprawl, slip, splash into the water, but manage to keep the rod tip high and the line tight. Somehow, the fish stays on the hook. It tears off upriver though, ripping yards from my whirring spool and zig-zagging madly across the oblivious run of the water.

I try to pull myself together and, panting and soaking, I play the fish for the next fifteen or twenty minutes or so, gaining in composure in a time-line roughly synonymous with the ache that gradually grows to a scream in my arm.

Finally, still under the gentle guidance of my ghillie and trying to pretend that my arm isn't about to fall off, I reel in the mighty fish as it lies acquiescent, shimmering, on the surface of the tea-stained waters. And it slips silently into the net.

That moment – when the fish is safely ensconced inside the gentle weave of a damp landing net, is a moment of finality; a ref's final whistle; an umpire's raised finger; an official end to hostilities. The battle is done.

After staggering, tripping and traipsing my way back onto the bank I stand in the weak Scottish sunshine and breathe heavily.

There are pats on the back and hearty handshakes. And the great gasping salmon lies before me, purple iridescence and silver chainmail etched with the faintest spots and trickeries of the light. Quite beautiful.

It's part of a multiproject, that glorious fish. For I am coasting through the Borders, dodging Reivers and discovering for myself that a trip far past these parts in search of greater Scottish wealth elsewhere could be construed as an opportunity missed.

It's a stunning part of the world. If you're after peat hags, red deer, the mournful cry of curlew or grouse, and glorious, royal-robed, sheep-flecked hills, you'll find them here.

But you'll also find the childhood playground of John Buchan, dells and woods, wandering streams of burning cold, and a taciturn but hospitable folk who know a good thing when they're in it.

❧

The next morning, I'm up bright and breezy and panting again, for this time I was striding atop one of those aforementioned purple tinged hills in the search for walked-up partridge.

A team of excitable assorted spaniels brave the unusual autumn heat to bustle through thick grass and stands of heather, and a team of just three guns – of which I was a sweaty one – staggered along behind.

Dog handlers and a motley crew of pickers-up fairly fly up the slopes, having done this three times a week all season and in all weathers. This is a cakewalk to these hardened souls. One resembles Catweazle, a thin, bewhiskered cove, all but unintelligible such was his thick, rolling timbre. But he too sallies forth with comically large strides, eating up the slope and his pale eyes – roofed o'er with great knotted thatch of a fading ginger unibrow – scan the horizon for dawdling dog or crouching partridge.

On this day of days, the burnished gold of an eagle splays out across the valley before us: an extraordinary-sized bird that lifts and soars on the warm air wafting from the rocky scree below. And every now and then, a covey of birds rockets from under the questing nose of a spaniel, breaking into flying formation and scattering in all directions of the compass.

I shoot several and miss many more, but the one I shall remember occurs towards the end of the climb when it is all I can do to raise the lightweight 20-bore I carry and sight across its thin twin barrels.

It's memorable because moments earlier I had nearly sprawled to a messy conclusion down an unseen drop, gazing as I was in admiration of the splendid scenery around me. I looked down in time to see my boot hanging precipitously over the beginnings of an uneven surface which ended in a nasty little drop into heaven knows what underneath a thin layer of heather below.

So now I turn smartly, wake myself up mentally and raise my legs a few inches higher upon each step as a form of punishment.

And then, with a whirr of its wings, the red-leg leaps up around twenty yards in front and curls away from me with astonishing speed. Before I know what I am doing, the gun is raised, the trigger pulled and the bird drops like a stone into the crevasse below. A single feather hangs on the still air to aerially mark the spot.

We have to stop the whole proceedings and employ the entire dog team and Catweazle himself to find that bird, for I want it badly for the next stage of my project.

And find it we do, eventually, and with it comes the end of a wonderful morning on the hilltops. I sink into the heather with a grateful sigh, swig from a coffee flask, lie back, warm barrels of my gun by my side, and stare up into the endless blue, watching thin clouds scud overhead.

Later that afternoon, after a trek down that was at least as bad as climbing up, Mike Roberts and I return to his little cave of invention.

The Ettrick Valley Smokehouse – a small, wooden clad building beside

> I sink into the heather with a grateful sigh, swig from a coffee flask, lie back, warm barrels of my gun by my side, and stare up into the endless blue, watching thin clouds scud overhead.

a dribbling tributary of the Tweed, hangs heavy with the ghosts of smokings past.

The great black smoker itself – forged by the mighty forearms of the village blacksmith – sits ominously in one darkened, tar-laden corner. Ochre glistens on every surface and a pile of fresh oak sawdust smoulders underneath its racks.

Mike guards his pre-smoke rub jealously, but I smell dill, and whiskey, and there's light brown sugar too and plenty of salt. Both the rich-hued flanks of my salmon and the darker breast meat of my partridge will be smoked today: the salmon cold, the partridge hot, with juniper, bay leaves, pepper and tart cider playing their part in its preparation for a few hours before being delicately licked by soft white tendrils of aromatic oak smoke.

And finally, as sun sets over the Tweed and an ectoplasm of mist begins to form in the valley hollows, we pour a healthy dram of whisky in thick, entirely practical stubby tumblers and sit down with a plate of fayre we've worked hard to bring to the table.

I can hear the occasional cough of deer up in the bristling hillsides as night falls, and I'll never forget the sweet tang of smoke on these meats. Their rich flavour coats the palate and I don't want to spoil the lingering flavour. So a light cigar is called for and I proffer my travelling humidor to Mike, who gratefully selects his weapon.

And I sit back with a mild, smooth, complex cigar from Highclere Castle, its turrets an unforgettable silhouette amidst rolling Berkshire countryside. It's famously where Downton Abbey was, and is, filmed. On another occasion, I'll tell you fondly of the afternoon I spent with Lord and Lady Carnarvon under the

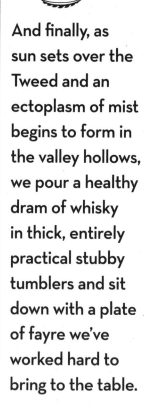

And finally, as sun sets over the Tweed and an ectoplasm of mist begins to form in the valley hollows, we pour a healthy dram of whisky in thick, entirely practical stubby tumblers and sit down with a plate of fayre we've worked hard to bring to the table.

shade of the magnificent Lebanese Cedar tree which stands sentinel in one corner of the grounds.

But for now, suffice to say that the Earl of Carnarvon, as well as tending to the estate and family seat, also makes a Nicaraguan cigar of note. I'm pleased to say both that he loves a cigar – and that the one carrying the name of his ancestral home is a fine one.

It's the right cigar for this occasion, entirely memorable in its delicate shroud of white pepper and hint of of leather. And the sun drops over the Borders, bringing dark to that spectacular landscape for a few more short hours. And the embers of our cigars glow on into the darkness.

And the sun drops over the Borders, bringing dark to that spectacular landscape for a few more short hours. And the embers of our cigars glow on into the darkness.

CHAPTER THIRTEEN

A Little More Nicaragua

TWO MAGNIFICENT PYRAMIDS, CLAD IN THE SOFTEST AND
RICHEST GREEN, ALL FLECKED WITH SHADOW AND SUNSHINE,
WHOSE SUMMITS PIERCE THE BILLOWY CLOUDS.

— *Mark Twain*

Back to School

It's never a good look, the red-faced, sweat-dripping one. Especially at breakfast. But Nicaragua will do that to you, especially if you have to move around at all.

And this morning, I do have to move around. Not dusting myself off for a marathon you understand, or taking part in an inspirational bout of spinning, but just getting on and off a bus. Everything seems hard work in the heat when you're used to throwing back the curtains to skies the colour of an elephant's backside.

So, by the time I step from the afore-mentioned bus in downtown Estelí, dust puffing up from the pavement as I disembark, there's already a telltale dark patch appearing on the shirt between my shoulder blades.

> It's never a good look, the red-faced, sweat-dripping one. Especially at breakfast.

While locals seem to carry off this look with ease, appearing to have just completed some healthy outdoorsy type of job, I look more like I've been thrashing through the undergrowth for a decade, narrowly avoiding the grasp of lurking serpents and fang-toothed mammals of every description.

It is this apparition, Dear Reader – minus the pith helmet – which greets the little old lady who stands meekly before the primary school, hands folded in front of her plain beige habit.

She is a nun, complete with wimple, sparkling eyes and a height of not more than five feet in heels. But behind those sparkling eyes is a flash of steel. And she needs it. For she is Principal of the Belén School in Estelí, which has been 'adopted' by some sections of the cigar community – most notably Sasja van Horssen's Longfiller Company of the Netherlands. His amazing Amsterdam store, Cigaragua, donates 10 per cent of every stick sold to the charity behind this little patch of dry earth. And as this little lady – Sor Purificación of the *Fe y Alegría*, 'Faith and Happiness' Christian charity – leads me around, I can see why.

Bright-eyed, bushy-tailed little ones abound, in spankingly smart uniforms and with the gleam of freshly brushed teeth. They grin as we enter their classrooms and proudly sing in Spanish to show off their skills. Their enthusiasm, cheeriness and sheer spirit of life is compelling. I can't help grinning inanely with them and they laugh at me, which then makes me laugh and boy, are we having fun all of a sudden.

These kids have very little – but the sad truth is that they are the lucky ones in cigar town. Statistics show that youngsters in Nicaragua's poorest areas – just like Estelí – spend as little as five years or less in mainstream education. That means before they've even reached their teens, many of them are out working to help their families make ends meet. From here, it is easy to fall into a life of drudgery – gangs, drugs, underage pregnancy or unemployment – and the cycle repeats itself, depressingly relentless in its monotony.

Sasja van Horssen's ProNica charity is determined to try and help break this cycle and last year handed over a cheque for in excess of £30,000. That may not sound a lot in Western terms, but it goes an awful long way in Estelí. It has bought equipment and paid for the building of new classrooms designed to be able to cope with older as well as younger students – so they can do some evening classes and continue to learn instead of being forced to work and onto the streets.

As the sun continues its assault overhead, my diminutive guide leads me to some scrub ground at the rear of the school, where a set of rusty goalposts have been hammered into the cracked, parched, cemented ground. I wouldn't fancy a sliding tackle on that, let me tell you. But this is something special at Belèn School.

'This,' Sor Purificación Gutierrez says proudly, with a grand sweep of her arm, 'is our new playground.'

There's some rickety play equipment which has seen better days – a wonky swing, old seesaw and the like. And the school is thrilled with it.

I am speechless.

There are cheerful adults busy cooking in the tiny kitchen; plates of steaming rice and beans, of course, but also some vegetables and of special joy to them, some sweet pineapples chunks for a treat. I'm invited to join them for lunch but am horrified at the idea. Every morsel is precious here and I am definitely not in need of their food. But I do gratefully accept a tiny wedge of pineapple.

In one small room, there are a sea of old Singer sewing machines and I'm wondering if a bit of old-fashioned sexism has raised its ugly head. I shouldn't have worried. Sor Purificación Gutierrez breezily announced that this is where both boys and girls are taught how to make do and mend; vital skills where buying new clothes is an impossibility for most.

There's a 'further education' classroom down one end of the school building, which demonstrates brilliantly how this charity and school are working in practical terms with the realities of the situation on the ground. This classroom is largely used for keeping older children in education; or for those whose life situations mean they simply have to leave school early to provide for their families.

Some of these kids get up early, walk to school, and study for a few hours before heading back out into Estelí to either help their parents in the fields or carry out their own jobs in town to get food on the table. In most towns in Nicaragua, these kids – as young as eleven or twelve sometimes – would be lost to the educational system. They'd effectively have to fend for themselves for the rest of their lives.

Fe y Alegría has a solution. In the evenings, these youngsters return to school for a few more precious hours of learning. Whether they're old enough to understand it or not, it's not too much of an exaggeration to suggest these few precious minutes each week may end up saving their lives.

The older students come too; the ones that have simply been unable to remain in school any longer. They too are given life skills and knowledge beyond the basics. To change their lives for the better, they need help; some learning of the world; they need people to look up to – and they need the likes of you and me.

These Nicaraguan familes are good people and they deserve better. I have two girls of my own and as I stand in the playground watching these youngsters, I can't help but appreciate that we all lead very different lives. Some are more fortunate than others through no fault of their own.

If you've bought this book – and I sincerely hope you haven't stolen it – then you are doing your bit to help these beautiful raven-haired kids and their families towards a better future.

Thank you.

You can't help it.

The minute you clap eyes on that great stretch of blue water that forms the Straits of Florida off Miami Beach, you can hear the music in your head.

You know the music I'm talking about. At least you do if you grew up in the 1980s. Crockett and Tubbs. Speedboats. Shoulder pads. Hot chicks in bikinis. It's *Miami Vice* time.

At least that's what I hear playing in my head the first time I clap eyes on the crashing sea opposite my hotel room when I throw back the curtains in the morning. And while I'm jetlagged as hell – my plane was delayed five hours at Heathrow and we didn't arrive at the hotel until 3 a.m. this morning – the first thing I do is grab my swimming shorts and head for the beach.

I have a bit of an obsession, you see. Because I'm usually as landlocked as it's possible to be in the UK, the sea is a great joy and mystery and whenever I get near it, I feel the urge to swim in its salty waters. As soon as possible.

Especially if I'm hungover or jetlagged or, worse still, both. I have this daft belief – that I'll recount to anyone who'll listen – that one day I'll reside by the briny blue and swim in it every day, no matter what the weather. Oh, and that if I could do this, I'd live to be one hundred.

This morning, the balmy, palm-fringed treats of Miami Beach are tossed in the skin-flailing eye of a storm, and the waters off the beach, instead of placid, serene blue, are an angry mottled green. And they gnash their teeth against the sand and spit spume into the air as I walk, goose-pimpled, around the outdoor pool, through the private gate and on to the sand, my head stuffed with cotton wool and my eyes bloodshot.

I get a couple of mild looks of surprise from early dog walkers. Then again, I suspect anything goes in Miami, although I am a shocking shade of Brit abroad.

Once I get to the water's edge, I let the surf rage around my calves. This forces me to notice that this delightfully refreshing saline Atlantic water is bloody cold. I decide that *actual* swimming might be quite a dangerous thing to do here anyway.

After all, great white sharks were spotted doing their thang not very far off these shallow waters just last week. I know because I made the mistake of checking on the internet.

I make do with bravely wading up to my thighs in the churning foam and letting the wind and seawater blow away my fatigue. Oh, and I also make do with getting smashed to the ground by a large wave and dragged up and down the beach until my thighs are scraped raw and my trunks have a couple of hand-fuls of coarse sand dumped in them. It's destined to be scattered around various hotel rooms, bathrooms, shower stalls and items of clothing during the next week or so. Welcome to Miami. This, and the hard rock of Crockett and Tubbs, is my initial welcome to this hot and sultry city, but what I'm really looking for while I'm here is Little Havana.

I make do with bravely wading up to my thighs in the churning foam and letting the wind and seawater blow away my fatigue.

It's a neighbourhood jam-packed with Cuban expats. And there's a street called Calle Ocho. That's the soul of Little Havana, right there. Cuban stores selling Cuban food; Cuban clothes shops selling cool linen guayaberas in bright, street-strutting colours; bars selling bucket loads of mint-infused mojitos; and every few steps, it seems, a cigar shop.

El Titan de Bronze is one of them. Its appearance is deceptive. It looks like just another 'mom and pop' brick and mortar cigar store, as they say in the US. And, in a reassuringly old-school, comfortingly practical sort of way, it is just that. But it is also the cigar shop and mini factory that spawned the mighty Willy Herrera. And he's a great guy.

Willy stands no taller than a wardrobe and is certainly only just a tad wider. And he used to be a bouncer in a nightclub. So you'll understand that when I get to meet him at the Drew Estate villa outside Estelí, Nicaragua – cricking my neck badly in an attempt to make eye contact – I'm in a bit of a Lilliputian-versus-Gulliver type of place.

But he's a jolly giant too: big piratical beard, perennial stogie smouldering in the corner of his mouth, and a sly grin never far away from his lips. Just don't rub him up the wrong way would be my advice. Or he might use your body parts in his next blend for Drew Estate.

It was Jonathan Drew who was, as he has so often been, first to spot potential and scoop Willy up as part of the D E team. Given carte blanche with the tonnage of tobacco that Drew has at its disposal, Willy was left alone for months on end so that he could have a play around.

And the resultant cigars – stunning *marques* like the Herrera Estelí – have proven Mr Drew's prophet-like powers once again.

Willy worked in the Titan shop for eight years, first learning how cool it was to hang there, then learning how cool it was to experiment with blends, and finally learning how cool it was to roll them, too. It seemed he had something of a knack.

> But he's a jolly giant too: big piratical beard, perennial stogie smouldering in the corner of his mouth, and a sly grin never far away from his lips. Just don't rub him up the wrong way would be my advice.

In the Drew Estate mansion overlooking scrubby plain and a dried-up riverbed in Estelí, I sit in the early morning cool and share a strong black coffee and a Norteño with Willy. It's another of his blends – strong and sweet, with a rich, dark San Andrés *maduro* (extra matured) wrapper. The big cigar looks like a toothpick in his hands and I watch each demonstrative wave of an arm like a concerned lumberjack watches an about-to-be-felled tree.

As usual, Willy is humility itself and we chat about this and that until I comment on the bird silhouetted on the cigar's label, its forked tail ending in two highly visible 'blobs'. Apparently it's a guardabarranco, Nicaragua's national bird.

'It's not seen that often round here,' rumbles Willy as he puffs on his Norteño. 'I've only seen them twice and I've been here six years.'

I blurt out: 'Oh, I saw one yesterday. It was diving among the trees down there.'

He fixes me with an eyeball roughly the size of my head. There is a long pause, during which he thoughtfully chews his cigar as if deciding which arm to tear off first.

Then – like a burst of Condega sunshine spilling through cloud cover – he grins wolfishly.

'Hey – that's great man. You must be lucky.'

And he raises his shovel hand for a high five. When his mitt swallows mine, it looks a bit like the sort of hand clap you might give your baby nephew. But we mean it and we are happy.

And he is right: I am lucky.

I'm sitting in the sun with one of the modern masters of blending, in a country blessed with all the right ingredients to make great cigars: soil, climate, topography, expertise, agronomy and, importantly, financial backing.

I'm here for a week or so with my good friend Scott Vines of Tor Imports.

I'm sitting in the sun with one of the modern masters of blending, in a country blessed with all the right ingredients to make great cigars: soil, climate, topography, expertise, agronomy and, importantly, financial backing.

He's responsible for most of the New World cigars that are imported into the UK these days, and over the years we've become good pals and travelling companions.

Drew Estate is a client of his – and here we are, learning how it's done first-hand. We landed yesterday and climbed aboard the Cigar Safari bus, our bags tossed onto the roof and secured, a box of Liga Privada No.9 passed round and a bottle of Flor de Caña Nicaraguan rum uncorked. An icebox of cold Toña beers lay in the front – and our journey began.

After several rowdy hours, a whole new genre of country/rock/blues/soul and funk under our belts, and with the pleasing buzz of rum and cigars in the air, we arrived at the Drew Estate compound.

It's literally that. The gates swing open, the gates swing shut behind you. And there is that famous mural by Jessi. The mural is a huge, colourful *Día de los Muertos* or Day of The Dead style piece of graffiti and the man behind it is the larger than life character that is Jessi Flores. Jessi was a punk getting into trouble on the streets when he first met Jonathan Drew. The pair hit it off. Now Flores gets paid instead of arrested for his graffiti and his work and originality are recognised the world over.

> ## The gates swing open, the gates swing shut behind you.

The phenomenon that is the Drew Estate 'compound' abounds with characters; in fact, it's a pretty Shakespearean place all round, with larger-than-life personalities, great back stories, plot twists and turns and some seriously weird language designed to leave you a little baffled. If you didn't know that MUWAT stands for My Uzi Weighs A Ton, then you do now. You're welcome. It's actually the name of a cigar, you know.

There's plenty more where that came from, too. D E likes to be different. Hell, if you stand still long enough, you're likely to get painted by Jessi and his crazy Subculture crew, now a full-blown design studio attached to D E. Youngsters from Estelí have come from poverty – like Flores himself – and found themselves inspired and invigorated by the liberating kaleidoscope of ideas, form, colour and expression that is the Subculture Studios. Jessi was the first of the talented waifs and strays that J D discovered. He's got a lot to answer for, that man.

The studio prides itself on being able to paint just about anything on just about anything. Which is why visitors on the Cigar Safari, who come down to learn about the business, take in the scenery and smoke more cigars in three days than Sir Winston did during the Second World War, bring assorted humidors, figurines, articles of clothing and more and hand them over to Subculture. The studio boys and girls weave their magic in mysterious ways...

CHAPTER FOURTEEN

Maldives

FOR SOLITUDE SOMETIMES IS BEST SOCIETY,
AND SHORT RETIREMENT URGES SWEET RETURN.

— *John Milton*

Have you ever done yoga?

Believe it or not, I'm a bit of a convert (actually, I reckon there's a book to
be written on cigars and yoga, but don't tell anyone because I think I might
write it).

At the end of your session – and especially a good, hard session, with
plenty of knee-shuddering lunges, gut-screwing twists, precarious balances,
and the odd inversion thrown in for good measure – there's a state of mindfulness reached that feels like you're floating. It usually only lasts a minute
or two before class ends, which is annoying, because I'd like to lie there, in a
state of trance, all day long.

There was a time when I'd drift straight off to sleep after a hard session
and be woken up by my own snoring and the giggles of the other yoga-goers.
Now, in the right state of mind, I can slip into a catatonic trance but remain
conscious. Sort of.

You lie, your energy spent. Your limbs feel as if they've been plucked off
and placed back together again – correctly. Your alignment and posture is
a revelation and your muscles are grateful for a period of relaxation after
a strenuous hour or so of mindful stretching. This blissful state, this out of
body experience, is, I think, what yoga is supposed to be all about. It feels, to
me, like lying on my back as a kid on a baking summer's day, and watching
clouds shift across an endless cobalt sky.

In those days, the universe was massive, time unimportant. Days lasted for ever, a week was a gulf in time beyond reckoning. New sights and experiences happened on a daily basis. The world was a strange and exciting place.

And for the first time in my life outside of a yoga class or childhood experience, that feeling of utter peace sank through me like a pebble dropped in a pond when I sat on the sands of a Maldivian island.

Warm, welcoming sunshine wraps its arms around me. The surf gently laps and surges, sparkling and inviting like a suggestively beckoning finger. The sand is powder, deep and warm underfoot. The gentle mix of colours – sky, aquamarine sea, the warm vermillion of the inside of your sun-splashed eyelids – all combine as an orchestra to soothe, calm, de-stress and reinvigorate.

Most of my time on Bolifushi Island is spent in this state of grace. The Jumeirah Vittaveli is one of the most extraordinary places on the planet.

When you tell people you're going to the Maldives, the general impression is that you're off to an idyllic island getaway for the rich and idle. You're not doing anything in particular; just going on an outrageously luxurious retreat – just because you can. And why the devil not, I say, if you can afford it?

Oh, I know many of the 1,500 or so islands of this archipelago nation have been created from a few grains of sand; I realise the country's record on human rights may leave something to be desired; I realise that you stand a heightened chance of bumping into one of those people who have more money than sense or good manners in such spots.

But it's not like you're going somewhere really naff, is it? Like Dubai, for instance.

Anyway, those who give knowing looks upon hearing the word Maldives can shove them right where the 365-days-a-year 30-degree-Celsius sun doesn't shine. For I've fallen truly, madly, deeply in love.

I arrive in this Shangri La, a sweaty, smelly, pale-faced Brit who wonders what on earth he was thinking, bringing his entire family on a trip to this sandy deposit in the middle of the Indian Ocean.

I had even gone to the trouble of making the whole exercise a surprise. Only once we jumped in our Heathrow-bound cab did I flourish a printed page of explanation of where we were going and what we had in store. I had told them to pack swimsuits, sunscreen, evening clothes and a smile.

But even that ridiculously romantic gesture felt like a waste of time as we bumped along backroads trying to avoid a gridlocked M1. The kids were bickering, the wife was fretting over some forgotten luggage, and I wondered sickly what on earth had possessed me. They read through the page of announcement with, what seemed to me, little enthusiasm.

Thankfully, we made our flight in plenty of time and flew from Heathrow to Colombo, Sri Lanka, where we sweated some more as we dashed from one side of the airport to another to catch another flight, which was suicidally tight for a connection. The girls were disorientated by the overnight flight: groggy and grumpy and astounded by the locals in the thronged airport who burped and farted loudly as they walked past as if it was the most natural thing in the world to do in public. Which it is, it seems, in Colombo.

My eldest, Grace, was further debilitated by the puking she'd felt compelled to indulge in just as we came in to land. My reverie upon descent was broken by a plastic cup thrown quite hard against the side of my head. My darling wife, on the other side of the aisle, was trapped next to a vomiting twelve-year-old with the seatbelt signs on and landing imminent. Quite what I was supposed to do about it I still haven't figured out, but I suppose it made her feel better. Grace's in-flight meal had made a surprise reappearance in her own lap. The poor passengers around her did their best not to join in the regurgitating fun.

I'm pleased to report the Sri Lankan Air staff were lovely; although their patented remedy of 7-Up and black pepper was not what my twelve-year-old was expecting. A trip to the toilet with her mother and a miraculous usage of the barely available non-soiled clothing we possessed, and we were soon dashing through Bandaranaike to catch our connecting flight to Malé. And one wonders why air travel with kids can be stressful?

The blast of humid air wasn't what Grace was hoping for on top of a queasy stomach; a massive queue curled away from us and we began to prepare ourselves for the inevitable fact that we were unlikely to get past sullen security guards in time. Especially as toga-wearing, shaven-headed Buddhist monks were seemingly waved through before everyone else. They even had their own marked seating areas in air-conditioned coolness, while the rest of us sweltered in godforsaken queues. I'm all for respecting men and women of the cloth, but I'll admit I had blasphemous daydreams of shaving my head, stealing a sheet and claiming I was a Holy man (how *do* you prove you're a monk?).

My thoughts were rudely interrupted by a rotund security guard who yelled to those of us on the connecting flight and ushered us through security. The screens overhead told us we were on last call – but once we realised this was more for show than anything else, we calmed and made the flight. We were loaded with ample supplies of sick bags and were in the air again once more.

By the time Malé, the capital, is reached, so is the end of our collective tether. Best part of twenty-four hours travelling, little sleep, time zones, kids: this is a match made in the deepest, darkest think tanks of Hell.

But then comes salvation in the form of a fridge-cold, air-conditioned waiting room. While the rest of the poor Joe Schmoes wilt in the sweaty heat, we are ushered inside the Jumeirah Vittaveli bubble of chilled serenity. Cold waters are handed round, sweets and nuts offered to tired palates. And then our boat arrives.

It's more yacht than boat. More high-powered speedboat, in fact, than yacht. In seconds, we're clear of the turquoise waters of the harbour and speeding into the deeper blue of the delightfully lashing sea.

A rooster tail flumes from the propellors as we fly and sickly eldest daughter discovers she's alive. She yells, 'Wahoo!' at the top of her voice and we grin at each other as briny spray mops our fretted brows and the wind blows away our air cabin blues. We've made it.

The island itself defies much flowery description. Once the boat docks (a drum-playing, smile-drenched party wait to welcome you), you take a short walk up the wooden jetty where chilled Champagne is thrust into your hand. Orchids spot the sandy walk to the houses, lodges and palaces beyond. This is island holidaying by CGI; the colours are so bright, the setting so perfect. At times during your stay at Vittaveli, it's all so preposterously magical, you feel like a dastardly Walt Disney executive has drugged and kidnapped you, shoved you in front of a blue screen and begun the most dazzling illusion known to man.

For the rest of that vaunted week, I barely wear shoes. For an Englishman, this akin to splitting the atom. And whisper it – I don't wear socks either. The sheer hedonism makes me light-headed thinking about it.

There are a variety of restaurants, bars, pit stops and hangouts you can frequent throughout your sun-kissed day. Just out of the sea and fancy some tapas and a cold beer with your toes still in the sand? No problem. If it's afternoon rain o'clock and you want to dive into shelter, take a fresh fruit cocktail and a vast selection of food choices on a walkway over the waves. There are hammocks slung here just over the water that occasionally give you a refreshing slap of surf. You can practise your golf swing by knocking a few balls into the Indian Ocean. But don't worry about littering – these balls are made of fish food which slowly disintegrates and gives a passing shoal a mouthful.

There are fish aplenty in these crystal waters. You'll regularly see rays and baby sharks from the shore as they patrol the warm shallows. One afternoon, while being treated to a soporific massage in one of several especially constructed chalets over the water, I'm astounded to find below the massage table a carefully sited window in the floor. As essential oils are eased into your relaxed skin, you can watch little sharks cruise past.

Sunsets are spectacularly colourful, with differing aspects from different vantage points on the island. You can walk or bike round Bolifushi in a few minutes, and as

There are fish aplenty in these crystal waters. You'll regularly see rays and baby sharks from the shore as they patrol the warm shallows.

carefully sized-up bikes are already lined up outside your lodge – complete with name tags on each – you can explore at your leisure. The soft hiss of compact sand under your wheels is pretty much the only sound apart from the ocean to accompany you.

Vittaveli's jewel is, of course, the sea. If you're not a scuba diver, don't fear. You'll have just as exhilarating an experience by donning a mask, snorkel and flippers, which you'll also be equipped with.

A splash or two from your chosen beach, of which there are many, you'll slip quietly over coral reef, where the action is. In just a few feet of water, mighty parrot fish dive and chomp. Octopuses are here, yet elusive. There are puffer fish, giant purple-lipped clams and a host of such brilliantly coloured smaller reef fish that your eyes will sting with the beauty of it all.

A few feet further on is what we termed 'The Abyss'. At first, we were nervous of this place where the warm shallow coral reef stops and the deep beckons. When I first drifted over its edge and peered down into the blackness, my breath came in ragged gasps and I flapped and splashed my way back to safer ground. Tess, our youngest at nine years old, saw a largish (harmless) shark on one of our first forays and had a similar panic. Grace, on the other hand, was swimming over and down The Abyss long before the rest of us plucked up the courage.

Yet by the end of the week, the thing we all want to do most is don our snorkelling gear and walk the few yards to our own stretch of golden beach and into the waves. If visibility is good – and that depends on a mystical confluence of tide, wind and current – hours slip past unnoticed as you cruise the surface and simply observe. One of the most relaxing and therapeutic things I've ever done.

Unlike, unfortunately, deep-sea fishing.

I've done my share of fishing over the years, as you've already learned in these pages. And the chance to board a huge, gleaming charter boat and head out into the Indian Ocean in search of sailfish or marlin is not to be missed. It means an early start and missing the morning snorkel. Quite a sacrifice.

But as the resort's general manager has invited me along, I think it wise to be there prompt at 6 a.m.

Except the same general manager and I were laughing and drinking Scotch at 2 a.m. the 'night before'. After a meal of staggering competency in the resort's French restaurant (there's a wine library here of some remarkable vintages, all stocked in carefully monitored conditions) we stole across to the Sautter Cigar Lounge. I've already introduced you to Laurence Davis, owner of Sautter of Mayfair, and suffice to say, having spent time on Vittaveli, he recognised the one thing missing was a superlative cigar location. So, he and Amit – aforementioned general manager – set about creating one.

It's a small space, beautifully furnished. Vintage cigars from the Sautter vaults have been shipped and stored. And here, with warm trade winds blowing beyond the Perspex lounge, with an expanse of sea in front and the very finest in libations to hand, Amit and I smoked a sensational Montecristo Edmundo – a biscuity, moreish, hefty smoke that sat comfortably in one hand, a glass of aged malt in the other. Just as we decided that we really should be getting some sleep ahead of our voyage in the morning, the heavens opened and it rained in a drenching, swirling downpour. Thunder boomed, lightning whip-cracked over the ocean and even umbrellas furled inside out in the surging wind. So, we poured another drink.

I eye Amit sourly the next morning after a wobbly bike ride to the marina. He eyes me sourly back. As the boat spouts diesel fumes we hold our counsel glumly and watched Bolifushi recede into the distance. We slug back two strong espressos each and perk up a little.

The gleaming white and chrome vessel throbs menacingly and bears us with purpose across waves which, as we pass further and further from shore, seem to grow in bravery. Soon they are white-topped menaces waiting for us to get just deep enough.

'Once we're past the reef, it's going to get rough,' says Amit, squinting at the horizon. I follow his gaze. Out there, in the great wet beyond, are lowering clouds of dense, dark foreboding.

We've barely slipped out of sight of the island when the first storm catches us. If we thought last night was wet, it was a sauna compared to this display. The boat pitches. The boat rolls. Even the nonchalant barefoot Maldivian crew leap for handholds as we are tossed from side to side. Amit and I laugh. At least at first. We couldn't be any wetter if we'd been in the ocean, so we laugh it off and hold on for dear lives. We are handed great fluffy towels but these soon become heavy with a mixture of rain and seawater.

We bravely battle on, four rods with lures running behind us trying to tempt some passing denizen of deep. One of the crew keeps trying to press Champagne on us. He's come prepared. There are cigars, bottles of Scotch, beer, sandwiches, cakes.

The first storm passes us and then the second descends. The deeper the water, the rougher the sea. Amit and I stop laughing.

We cling on for dear life, then decide that we'll be better off inside. A fatal decision.

I don't know why, but once inside the confines of the cabin – and it is a luxurious cabin if ever I've seen one, complete with bar, TV and comfy sofas – the game changes completely. Within a minute or two I begin to experience a strange sense of curling, creeping nausea. Sweat collects at the nape of my neck. Generally speaking, I have good sea legs. I've been fishing with oyster and lobstermen and took a trip with the Royal National Life-guard Institute once down in Cornwall at the tail end of a storm. Then, all I could see were grey roiling seas all round, but while the press officer and the crew fell to sickness, I remained remarkably sanguine about the whole affair.

But I now realise the sea has caught up with me. It has circumnavigated my defences and sneaked up. We are in deep water, heading to deeper – and I am seasick.

'Champagne?' enquires the cheerful crewmate. 'A sandwich?'

I lurch aside. Amit is looking stony-faced through the window into the bleakness beyond. I breathe a long, shuddering breath and he turns to look at me. He's a dark-skinned man, but he looks decidedly pale to me.

We look at each other for a long, uncertain moment. There is no way I can ask them to turn around. The trip has been arranged specifically for me; they've laid on a feast fit for a king; we have the whole day at our mercy to fish, have a drink, enjoy a smoke.

'Turn around,' Amit drawls above the noise of the engine and the squall outside. 'We're going home.'

> **But I now realise the sea has caught up with me. It has circumnavigated my defences and sneaked up. We are in deep water, heading to deeper – and I am seasick.**

I've seldom been so relieved to hear those words. I try to make some token protest but it dies on my lips.

'You too, eh?' I say. He nods glumly and we steer tortuously back to shore.

It is just a day later when I spring from bed with an air of joie de vivre, choosing to forget my ignoble flight from the waves just hours before. Once back on terra firma, I recovered remarkably quickly and within an hour of touching dry land felt well enough for a spot of tapas and a cold beer on the beach, happy to observe the sea from a distance rather than imperil myself upon it.

But there's no fool like an old fool, so they say. Today I am going one step further on the sea equation. I'm going *under* it.

I've never scuba-dived in my life. Hours of underwater nature footage, an obsession with sharks (see earlier *Carcharodon* adventures) and a rising panic at the sight of deep, ever-darkening waters and what lies beneath had convinced me scuba-diving wasn't top of my bucket list.

I've never shown any real enthusiasm to release my inner Jacques Cousteau. But Jumeirah Vittaveli is nothing if not liberating; every waking hour is laced with a 'can do' attitude. Fancy picnicking on your own desert island, glugging Champagne with nary a speck of land in sight? Done. Fancy dining in your own private teppanyaki restaurant, with the resort's head chef personally whipping up a seafood extravaganza, your children employed as his sous chefs? *Pas de probléme* (thanks, Frances).

When you've been here a while, you begin to believe your own press, I'm sorry to say. And so, I insouciantly sign up for a day's scuba-diving course with the resort's young marine biologist. She's a tanned young Brit living the dream and we spend some time going through the basics of breathing apparatus, safety protocols and the like. We walk into the tepid water at the beach's edge to practise. And later that afternoon, we are aboard a skiff, heading seawards once more, this time to a wreck. Untethered from precious land, my bravado subsides. I begin to question the wisdom of this successive oceanic adventure. There's a reason I've spent the previous forty-three years without feeling the need to submerge myself in deep water on the other side of the world.

Too late.

We arrive. The water is calmer today, thank goodness, but visibility is crap. Which makes a huge difference to your dive experience, I discover. Not least because the majesty of the sea and its denizens are masked from you by a haze of cloudy, sandy particles; but also because as you cannot see properly, you are more on edge; less sure of what's around you; less able to settle down; and in my case, more liable to breathe quicker and use up your tank of oxygen faster.

We don't descend far – I believe the prescribed limit for first dives is something like twelve metres – but it's plenty far enough for me. Using a thick rope tied to the sunken prow of the ship, we pull ourselves into the depths, my guide's flippers disappearing in the murk in front of me. I'm not enjoying this.

Water seeps into my mask and begins to burble around, stinging my eyes. The natural human urge is to panic. It's hard to fight a natural urge. I use the technique shown to me on shore; blowing air into the face mask to force out the water. It works; sort of. I fight down my rising panic, respond to the inquisitive 'okay'? signal from my dive buddy and on we go.

It occurs to me that if I do flap, panic and inevitably lurch for the surface – for that is what every atom in your body tells you to do when in trouble underwater – I will cause potentially irreparable harm to myself. The Bends is not a trifle that can always be easily solved with a session on another oxygen tank. It strikes home to me that to get in trouble down here – even this relatively shallow dive – is to court death. Perhaps I should have given this more due consideration as the sun kissed my shoulders and the sand tickled my tootsies on the beloved, safe, tranquil and familiar world above.

Too late.

Perhaps I should have given this more due consideration as the sun kissed my shoulders and the sand tickled my tootsies on the beloved, safe, tranquil and familiar world above.

We go on. I hadn't considered currents down here, but they exist and pull and push me in a way I'm not expert enough to fully control. I roll and flip, clonk into passing coral, find it hard to descend far enough despite the weights attached to my belt. A grey hulk looms out of the gloom. The ship has been down here for decades and looks the part: eerie and lonesome, unshaven with its beard of underwater algae, pocked with the acne of mollusc and the blemish of darting fish.

Now I have a stern word with myself, for the panic is rising in me and I know that if I give in to it, there will be hell to pay. This dive will only last a few minutes. Another thirty or forty minutes at the most. Put up with the salty water sloshing in your mask; breathe slowly and deeply; follow the expert and get through it. We descend to the hull.

Here, the dive's only true magical moment happens for me. My instructor takes my hand and guides me to a small open hatch, placing my palms on the rim and signalling for me to hang on. I ignore images of lurking moray eels and patrolling tiger sharks and acquiesce.

We sit, silently suspended in saline. I look at her questioningly. And she points.

From the corners of the gaping hatch, tiny transparent shrimp emerge, their outrageously long feelers questing through the air towards the milky pale hands that have arrived on their doorstep.

They are ghostlike, tiny wraiths with tiger stripes. And they timidly tickle their way onto the backs of my hands and begin to diligently nibble (if nibble is the correct word). They dance across my skin in a delicate ballet. I break into a grin inside my mask.

> They dance across my skin in a delicate ballet. I break into a grin inside my mask.

The rest of the dive is a cloudy blur, to be honest. We reach the seabed and scoot along, searching nooks and crevices for creatures great and small. Plenty of big fish loom and recede in the darkness. There's the occasional excited gesticulation from my guide when she spots something my poorly trained eye can't make out. But I get through the rest of the dive without mishap. I can only leave to your imagination the feeling that sweeps over me once I've clambered back on board, been helped out of my suddenly weighty dive gear, been wrapped in a towel and handed a hot drink. The sun dips as we speed home. I've done it. I've scuba-dived. I don't feel it's something I need to do again.

Not so the snorkelling. That remains a smash hit in the Hammond palatial lodge. The girls have their own upstairs suite, complete with his and hers (or hers and hers) showers. We have a plunge pool, a balcony, a hammock, various chairs and sofas and our own private beach. The fridge is stocked with all one could desire. Icy air con pours from every room. On our last day, we are all quiet, heavy of heart. Never have we been on a trip like this. We snorkel fiercely, knowing it's our last chance, and are rewarded by the flapping flight of a turtle arcing over the abyss and away into the great blue beyond.

We dine like we've never dined before, spoiled to the point of speechlessness by the thoughtfulness and care of others on our last special night. As stars speckle overhead and my exhausted girls collapse among their Egyptian cotton to dream of the deep, I crack a cold beer from the fridge and walk – still no shoes and socks, folks! – on to 'my' beach where hundreds of nocturnal crabs scurry across the sand. The waves crash and palm trees salute in the stiff, warm breeze. I light up a La Sagrada Familia – a brand owned by my German friend Tom Mulder and made by the good folks at Joya de Nicaragua. It's a home run of a cigar: dark and subtly sweet like a wedge of moist, rum-sozzled Christmas cake.

We dine like we've never dined before, spoiled to the point of speechlessness by the thoughtfulness and care of others on our last special night.

I breathe a melancholy sigh, both grateful for what we've had and sad that we will no longer have it. Bolifushi truly is paradise on earth; not least because of the wonders that nature has bestowed upon it, but also because of the extraordinary level of love that goes into making each and every stay something sensational and unique. For that to work, you need great people.

They are here in abundance. Smiles and laughs are commonplace; nothing is too much trouble. Dream what you can. On Bolifushi, they'll make your dreams come true.

I sit quietly and listen to the ocean, and await the morning boat back to Malé.

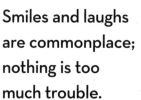

Smiles and laughs are commonplace; nothing is too much trouble. Dream what you can.

CHAPTER FIFTEEN

Munich

THE GERMANS ARE THE MOST PHILOSOPHIC PEOPLE IN THE
WORLD, AND THE GREATEST SMOKERS: NOW I TRACE THEIR
PHILOSOPHY TO THEIR SMOKING. SMOKING HAS A SEDATIVE
EFFECT UPON THE NERVES, AND ENABLES A MAN TO BEAR THE
SORROWS OF THIS LIFE (OF WHICH EVERYONE HAS HIS SHARE)
NOT ONLY DECENTLY, BUT DIGNIFIEDLY.

— George Borrow

M ist swirls around me in a vortex and my heels echo hollowly on the
cobblestones of this fine old town.

Somewhere in the distance a church bell tolls, muffled, indeter-
minate. Shapes loom and recede in the fog; shadows and halos of streetlamps
fuzz and pass into cloud.

I feel like Harry Lime in Vienna – eyes forever straining into a muddied
future; trailed by old ghosts.

Munich on a dank, cold, winter night is romance personified. Its grand
buildings shimmer with light; the occasional snowflake drifts nonchalantly to
burn on uneven cobble. Each road seems to lead to an alleyway; a staircase; a
furtive bar; a secret church.

Here, among the Louis Vuitton shops and the stores selling expensive
and useless handbags and shoes, is a strange mix of the old and the new, the
sacred and profane. There is new money aglow here, yet central Munich is
awash with old money too. It's all around you in the stature of the buildings;
the colossal and stunning opera house; the mansions along the expansive
Strasse where former kings, queens and courtiers carried on.

And here, as I pass the opera house, tonight hosting *Otello*, and dodge
German traffic and passing trams, I finally recognise what I'm looking for,
rising impressively out of the mist. The mighty Zechbauer building.

It stands astride an entire block like a colossus and is owned – as is the rest of the block – by the Zechbauer family, a dynasty of outrageously successful businessmen and women. They are makers of new tech, purveyors of the old and creators of this famous old tobacconist which now stands before me, unchanged since its doors proudly opened in the year 1830. In old pictures, the Zechbauer building looks just the same as it does tonight. Only the faded black and white images of pedestrians in period dress give the game away: a Prussian helmet here, a pinafore dress or sturdy laced-up boot there.

Oak-panelled boardrooms exist in the upper echelons of the mighty building; below is the beautiful old retail shop, where original blue and white tiles mingle with the ancient shelves and the smells of centuries of shelf-stocked snuff and tobacco.

I can't help imagining Munich as it might have been when it was originally built – an homage to the wealth and taste of the Bavarian court. It's named after the Benedictine monks who first settled here, building their monastery beside the River Isar and founding the site which would become one of the world's most prosperous – and pleasant – cities.

It didn't start that way. Much of what is now central Munich was marshland and it took considerable engineering skill, drainage, digging and no doubt a not inconsequential torrent of Bavarian bad language to reach the stage where civility could have been said to set in.

Succeeding monarchs set out to immortalise their blueprint on the city. It's why you'll find Maximilianstrasse and Ludwigstrasse, Leopoldstrasse and more; each avenue added a layer and a style, from opulent grandeur to garlanded French fancy. The city grew and sprawled and its architectural splendour evolved, layer upon layer.

Night comes early in the cold of a winter's afternoon here, and by the time early teatime rolls around, it's been a long day since my early hours' wake-up call and cross-country trip to the airport.

There's nothing more welcoming than an appropriately lit hotel lobby. First impressions really count here – in my experience, you can generally get a really

There's nothing more welcoming than an appropriately lit hotel lobby.

good opinion of a hotel and its ambience, attitude and style within the first twenty seconds of walking through the front door for the first time.

The Munich Kempinski passes this test with flying colours.

'Mr Hammond?' a concierge asks the moment I cross the threshold. I reply in the affirmative.

'I thought so, sir. We've been expecting you. Would you like a glass of water?'

This is an unexpected but very welcome question. I've only been travelling a few hours, but nothing dries like air travel, and after a train ride and a brisk walk through Munich town centre with my overnight bag I am indeed rather parched. Very thoughtful. Then the coup de grâce.

'You're something to do with cigars, aren't you, sir? I thought I recognised your face.'

Now I'm sure this is out of politeness; that, being an excellent concierge, this gentleman was asked to look out for my arrival and had the forethought and time to look up my details and mugshot beforehand. But it's rather flattering to one's ego to be recognised the second you step into a five-star hotel. I stand a little taller in the lobby.

I'm shown to my suite throughout the wandering corridors of this massive old building, which was built as a plaything and later became an internationally famed restaurant. It has housed a grand hotel for many years now, under the stunning cupola depicting the four seasons in the vestibule, the great and the good of Munich share coffee, gossip, a glass and the chance to show off their wealth.

My peaceful, modern room has more light switches than a naval commander could navigate and a monstrous bed of yawn-inducing comfort.

There's a very cosy bar in the hotel, where stools nestle conspiratorially close to, and slightly above, the barman. And with a cold, frothy local Pilsner in hand let me lead you, Dear Reader, across the aforementioned vestibule, up a scant few steps and into an enclave of peace and civility. For here, the mighty Zechbauer dynasty has opened a modest store of high-end cigars – and best of all, a magnificently opulent cigar lounge.

Mirko Pettene, Managing Director of Zechbauer Cigars, and the 'primus inter pares' of German tobacconists, meets me here to show off the space he has helped to create.

A reclaimed English marble fireplace occupies one wall – a large mirror hiding a flatscreen TV in the other. Ornate silverwork scrolls across both walls and on closer inspection, it becomes apparent they are covered in over-laying tobacco leaf. Now that's what I call wallpaper.

It's a lovely, clubbable spot, but not in the least bit snooty; while I'm there, I strike up a conversation with the table next door and we make friends for the remainder of my weekend stay. Well-known football players, actors and politicians slide innocuously in and out of this grand hotel – I sit opposite one former Premier League football star over schnitzel one evening.

Mirko joins me later for another slightly spooky stroll around mist-covered Munich, pointing out the spots of local history that I would have merrily passed by in my ignorance. Such as the statue of a lion, where everyone stops to rub one paw, an act said to bring them luck. The foot in questions is shiny worn and we both stop to give it a further polish and say our prayers to the God of lions' feet.

And Mirko leads me around one or two famous Munich beer halls, with their great foaming steins of German beer, and plate after plate of the most incredibly heavy food. About 99.9 per cent of which seems to include pork in its formative ingredients.

I thought the Spanish ate a lot of ham, what with their love for the *Ibérico*, the acorn-fed *bellota* ham, sliced translucent thin and so larded with fat it curls and melts on your tongue. But no one comes close to the Germans. Pork knuckle, pork schnitzel, *wurzt*, white pork and veal sausages, smoked ribs, pork roasted in beer sauce, sausage, sausage and extra sausage with cheese… It's exhausting just thinking about it and impossible to avoid, so grit your teeth and get piggy. Bavaria is old Germany: cold, hard winters, fur coats, warm hats, wild boar, big moustaches. Pork-eating aplenty. No room for lily-livered Brussel sprout-eating here. Dive in.

As evening lengthens, Mirko and I part company for the time being and I tread my echoing steps to yet another sacred space, hidden within cloistered walls amid another rat run of seeming dead ends. Tonight, this tastefully lit, vaulted space is holding a Mozart recital and I can't resist handing over my forty euros and taking a seat. You have to marvel at how civilised Germans are. I watch this peaceful space fill up with twenty-somethings, the occasional youngster, white-haired gentleman and carefully tailored older ladies, who talk quietly and settle down to enjoy an evening's entertainment. In a cosmopolitan city like Munich, recitals like these are commonplace, but it feels special to me, the perfect way to end a day exploring the small cultured city centre. After a brief, but reassuringly familiar tune-up, a glorious cascade of sound from violin and double bass fills the room.

This would be a perfect cigar moment, I muse as I close my eyes and let the music wash over me, soothing tired feet, easing travel tensions and the spiky energy one always carries when navigating a new city. Of course, simply lighting up in public is not possible these days, but I don't mind. I simply relax. And wonder how the world might just be a nicer place for us all if more people were able – and willing – to spend an hour or two enjoying evenings such as this.

༄

The Zechbauer building by daylight is just as impressive as in its evening attire – this a.m., it's dressed in grey formal morning suit and adopting the air of a benevolent uncle.

While the cigar shop on the ground floor offers old-world customer service and good old-fashioned indulgence, the rest of the building is divided into posh shops – Longchamp, Prada and the like – and high-ceilinged offices.

Today, the tobacconist hosts a cigar tasting. Customers can drop in for a social, try a smoke and talk to an ambassador of the chosen brand to learn where and how each particular cigar is made. After an agreeable couple of hours, off they go to finish their shopping, buy some more pork or something similar – and another batch of lovers of the good life come bowling in through the door.

Once again, it's a wonderfully civilised way to meet friends, mingle with the throngs in the city centre and wile away a few hours of your weekend. There's a definite theme developing here.

The *cigar du jour* today is the Balmoral Añejo XO Oscuro. While I politely listen to the brand ambassador's excellent explanation of the cigar and its origins, I already know it well. I smoked this cigar – and a few more besides – with its creator, Boris Wintermans, when I visited Royal Agio's state-of-the-art eco factory on the outskirts of Eindhoven.

Agio is an old company, young at heart. Boris is the latest in a line of Wintermans' to steer the company that once had hundreds of rollers making small dry Dutch cigars on the same site. These days, using an established network of the world's best tobacco growers, Boris blends small productions of exquisite cigars. He's as passionate a cigar man as I've met and I'd like to think that not too far down the line, my adventures may lead me out with him somewhere in the world inspecting the latest harvest of grade-A leaf.

But now I'm reluctantly forced to leave the warm fug of Zechbauer and step out into a Munich which has the pinched blue look of real cold. Snow is falling as I retrace my steps past the Staatsoper, the Kempinski, the show shops and the beer halls and begin the train journey back to the airport.

This is the last trip of the year for me, ending weeks of seemingly constant travel, and I'm weary. Back in Blighty, I manage to leave my bag on yet another train, minutes from home and the opportunity to pack the damn thing away in a cupboard for a precious few weeks.

But that minor calamity awaits. Now, I sit in the window seat as the city recedes in the background and the frost-nipped fringes of Bavarian countryside slide by. Plots of bristling woods, no doubt fine accommodation for generations of wild boar families; high seats in the corners of every large field; functional, dispassionate rail stations dotted all the way down the line; a swift and exactly timed run into the surprisingly large sprawl of Munich airport.

This final leg on the way home proves to be a delightful blend of old and new; chrome shine and burnished wood patina. An appropriate way to draw a close to my latest travelling adventure and speed home to my much-missed loved ones.

There's just time to enter the clean, airy and, of course, very civilised smoking room within the airport. What a pleasure to find such a thing. It's neither the colour of an old man's underpants, nor does it smell like them – unlike virtually every other airport smoking room it's been my displeasure to discover over the years. This one is well lit and tastefully decorated, with plenty of seats and charge points for the ubiquitous mobile devices all travellers clutch with them fiercely these days. There's even a good system of ventilation, which is a godsend. For while I love a smoke (and the aroma of freshly burned tobacco) the smell of stale smoke – particularly of the cigarette variety – is disgusting.

This afternoon, I'm aware I'm dog-tired. I've loved every minute of the adventures which form the basis of this book. But today I feel each and every one of them, stretching back over a quarter of a century, weighing heavily upon me. In order to get the book finished in time for my publishers, I've had to wedge in a huge amount of travel in the past few months, jumping from plane to train, crossing continents and nipping from scene to scene in a wonderful but somehow discombobulating blur of places, people and events. When I reach this general state of bewilderment, I'm even more likely than normal to act like a zombie and leave bags behind, forget taxis, turn up on the wrong day for planes and the like. So I am trying to be extra careful of my own potential idiocy. I check my passport for the umpteenth time, make sure my bags are still with me (oh, the irony) and dig out another Balmoral Añejo XO while I wait for my flight to be called. The cigar is rich and dark, like a slice of malt loaf, and it's the perfect accompaniment to a black coffee and a baguette filled not, thankfully, with pork, but a simple cheese and salad. My stomach rejoices.

The cigar adds an underlining punctuation to Operation Munich with a flourish. And it brings to end the gamut of my travels for now. I hope there will be plenty more to regale you with in the future. Thank you for reading – happy travels – and long ashes to you all. Until next time.

Thank you for reading – happy travels – and long ashes to you all.

CHAPTER SIXTEEN

Great Places I've Smoked a Cigar

IF YOU CAN'T SEND MONEY, SEND TOBACCO.

— George Washington

This isn't meant as an exhaustive list, nor a rehash of what I've already put down on paper for you, but as an extra added bonus, if you like. These are some of my favourite and most interesting places to smoke a cigar, should you be so inclined to follow in my footsteps – if only for a nose around an interesting area. They are not in any order or in any way similar, on the whole, and they dot around the world in my mind like little red markers on a sprawling war-room wall map.

They all share something in common, quite apart from being a great spot to enjoy a smoke. They also happen to be interesting and unusual places, and worthy of your attention even if you're as likely to light up a hand-rolled cigar as you are to don a bearskin helmet and dance the funky chicken in the light of the silvery moon (great fun if you've never tried it).

Look 'em up if you're in the area and tell 'em I said sent you.

Davidoff of London

I can't help thinking of this little oasis of civilisation in the heart of wealthy and often affected Mayfair with a grateful imaginary sigh. Since I first got to know Eddie and Edward Sahakian a good number of years ago now, it's become a resting spot and a solace for me – a man not used to the hurly-burly of the daily London commute.

I still find it hard to climb aboard train, Tube, bus and taxi – often all in the same day – to get to, from and round and through the great sprawling metropolis that is the modern-day city. I try to time my comings and goings to avoid the worst of it, when literally millions are on the move – all at the same time. But sometimes, by sheer bad luck, or by other people's diaries, I am caught up in the remorseless pull of the commuting tide and I get sucked into the maelstrom to stand, crushed, sweaty and humiliated on the Tube, cheek by jowl with other people who have as much desire to be in enforced, up-close intimacy with me as I do with them; to curse and get ill-tempered and tut when my travel plans are undone by forces greater than my own; to walk round and round, until footsore and thoroughly miserable, looking for an address I thought would be a short distance and easy to find.

And on occasion, when I've been able, I've made a beeline for the little shop on the corner of St James's Street and Jermyn Street, which glows like a beacon and carries a multitude of exquisite accessories, ornaments and trinkets for the like-minded. Here, often accompanied by Edward or Eddie, or on high days and holidays, sometimes joyously both, I have enjoyed many a great cigar, event or simply moments of peace. Thank you, gentlemen, and may there be many more to come.

www.davidoffLondon.com; Tel: (+44) 207 930 3079; 35 St James's Street, London, SW1A 1HD

Cigaragua, Amsterdam

Another 'Aah' and exclamation of breath when I think of this little colourful, well-lit cave of glories.

Amsterdam is such a lovely city, criss-crossed as it is by its picturesque canals, like strands of a spider's web all leading inexorably to the centre. The spider at the centre of this tortuous analogy is Sasja van Horssen, who is mentioned elsewhere in these pages as the man behind the ProNica charity, which has raised *a lot* of money for underprivileged children in Nicaragua.

Sasja's not everyone's cup of tea; he's up front and he speaks his mind and – like many other Dutch folk it's been my pleasure to know over the years – I reckon he's also ever so slightly barmy. He makes me laugh. I met him at a tobacco trade event at Nottingham years ago and the day was so stultifyingly dull, we decamped and found a nice bar overlooking the River

Trent and Nottingham Forest Football Club, a stone's throw from Trent Bridge Cricket Ground. We proceeded to spend the rest of the afternoon smoking cigars and swapping stories and making wild and impulsive plans.

That's another trademark of Sasja – but in his case, he brings them to fruition. Hence Cigaragua. It's the only shop of its kind in the world, selling purely cigars made in Nicaragua, so firm is the owner's belief that this country is the future of the hand-rolled cigar.

A large, state-of-the-art walk-in humidor, a very cool entrance mural and a clean and attractive sampling lounge means this is a must-stop on your visit to the land of the bicycle and windmill. (Seriously, watch out for those bikes; *everyone* rides one, from little kids on the way to school to octogenarians off to shuffle around the market. They have dedicated lanes on all public roads and you WILL get knocked over if you don't keep your wits about you!)

Here you can wile away a couple of hours before you need to head to the airport to catch your plane, or plan your visit to the Van Gogh Museum just across the road. You'll get great advice from enthusiastic cigar guys and some free WiFi and good coffee. And the chance to chat with some interesting folk. You might even bump into me.

www.cigaragua.nl; +31 020 773 5302; Van Baerlestraat 56, 1071 BA Amsterdam

James J Fox of London

Another in the little set of exquisite cigar shops in this 'Royal Mile' of Mayfair, J J Fox (as I've mentioned earlier) has a hallowed history of supplying the great and the good.

But what I haven't really banged on about is the upstairs sampling lounge, where one can select a cigar from the immaculate humidor downstairs and settle comfortably to enjoy it. The former smoking room was a little old box with some rickety furniture, if I'm honest, but it always attracted a rum gaggle of characters and was great fun to spend an hour or so in if you happened to be passing.

The new lounge is on an entirely different plane. Lovingly equipped with coffee machine (free), WiFi (free), couches and armchairs (free), and a bounteous selection of rare, aged and modern cigars (free – dream on), this is a classic example of how to make a place appealing, comfortable and equally able to host an evening event, a business meeting or an afternoon-off extravaganza.

There are monthly events held here, from celebrations of Sir Winston's birthday to explorations of brands and pairings with rums and whiskies. Another cigar joint of gold-medal standard.

www.jjfox.co.uk; email: freddie@jjfox.co.uk; Tel: +44 (0)207 930 3787; 19 St James's Street, London, SW1A 1ES

Club Mareva, Split

Croatia is a wonderful melting pot of nations and cultures. And the long, warm summers and temperate winters make it a wonderful spot to visit at any time of the year. The Adriatic Sea is a delight – so mineral-rich you can hear it fizz and crackle when you dunk your head to cool off every now and then. The food is sublime – plenty of seafood – a decadent take on Italian cuisine mixed with something a little more mysterious from further east. Power after power decided Split was for them in bygone years – so the nature and influence of its people and their cuisine is equally diverse, creating a wonderfully exotic and different city just a stone's throw from mainland Italy itself. No wonder the Roman Emperor decided this was the ideal spot for his summer palace.

I'm not quite sure how Marko Bilic did it; but then again, he can be a persuasive so-and-so. Marko is the man behind Club Mareva. And he somehow persuaded the powers that be to let him open Club Mareva in a UNESCO world-heritage building bang in the middle of Split. I told you he was persuasive.

Marko is also the man behind the World Cigar Smoking Championship – which travels the world seeking the smoker who can make a small cigar (actually a size known as *mareva*, funnily enough) last the longest. A strange concept, for sure, but a good excuse for cigar nuts from around the world to get their heads together in exotic locations and have some fun. I've joined Marko for his adventures in Split and can recommend you do the same. He's a gentleman and his club is delightful: very friendly and a great place to enjoy a cigar and a chat. It's a private club, so you'll need to be a member or a guest of one to get in, but if you happen to be in Split, I suggest you make contact with Marko and tell him I sent you. My friend will look after you.

www.clubmareva.com; Main City Square, Split

Robert Graham 1874

It's ironic that Robert Graham – a store that was invented and remains a business based around tobacco products – can no longer allow its customers to sample its excellent wares anywhere on the premises.

That's the case in Scotland, anyway, but at least in the two English stores, in Cambridge and London, more amenable rules apply. Here, you're welcome to pull up a chair, choose a dram from a sensational selection, select a suitable cigar from a walk-in humidor stuffed with good things, and enjoy some warm peace and quiet.

The smoking ban in Scotland is doubly a shame, for if you can get out of the weather – a very big if – this is a tremendous place to enjoy a cigar. The great, rugged outdoors is never far away, yet the sophistication and energy of cities like Edinburgh and Glasgow give you a different perspective to many of their nearby European counterparts. Edinburgh particularly is a spectacular city – watched broodingly as it is by the castle on the hill – with world-class bars and restaurants and atmosphere to sample.

But I have a sneaking admiration for Glasgow too. It's real, lived in, always exciting. The Robert Graham store here has been around for ever, serving the great and the good their pipe baccy, cigars and drams for the weekend. Billy Connolly has been popping in here for a cigar for years and store manager Linda has a great line in banter.

Robert Graham is owned these days by Scotsman Steve Johnstone, who's brought a superb new line of cigars to the market. Tobacco Lords – named after the famous city fathers of years gone by, who controlled the world trade in tobacco from this crucial port, are a great value, well-made cigar. It's blended and rolled by the artisans at Joya de Nicaragua, so if you're passing a store, grab one as you go.

www.robertgraham1874.com

Havana House, Windsor

Paresh Patel is something of rarity in the cigar business. He's a cigar owner who likes to stay in the background. Most prefer to be up front and centre – and there's nothing wrong with that, after all – but unless you make an effort to find out, you won't know Paresh is involved in a string of great cigar shops across affluent parts of England and Wales. Indeed, I'd known him for years, and bumped into him at countless cigar events, both here and abroad, before we really got to know each other.

A shrewd operator with a knack for running a great cigar store as a tight ship, Paresh has select shops in Windsor, Bath, Cardiff, Hove, Oxford, Reading and Stratford-upon-Avon: a stable of lovely cities that no other UK cigar merchant can match.

I like to drop into the Windsor store. It's not fancy or grand – just a proper cigar store in a lovely, lovely town. The River Thames sweeps majestically through this old place, past meandering streets and pleasant shops. (Although I once did get a whopping parking fine here for being ten minutes late, and that was after paying something extortionate like £20 for the privilege of parking there for the day. Traffic wardens should be condemned to the fiery pits of Hell, in my mind. But I suppose that's a story for another time.)

But Havana House Windsor just feels right, this little shop with a hideaway sampling lounge at the back. And if you're lucky enough to visit when the weather is being kind, you can select something delicious from the humidor (and Paresh knows a good smoke when he sees one; he's sole importer for a number of excellent New World brands, including RoMa Craft, owned by my pal Skip Martin – his cigars are *awesome*).

Then you can nip out back to a pretty little courtyard – where there also happens to be an excellent small coffee shop – and light up to enjoy your chosen time of serenity.

It feels right too, that places such as Windsor, Bath, Stratford, etc. have a damned fine tobacconist to keep them entertained. The shop in Cardiff is even known as the Bear Shop by the locals and has been for decades. Why, you ask? Because there's a giant stuffed bear in there, of course. And boy he, and plenty of other customers from that land of rolling hills, enjoy the relaxation offered by a fine, hand-rolled cigar.

www.havanahouse.co.uk

Havana House, Windsor, 52 Windsor Royal Station, Windsor, Berkshire, SL4 1PJ; Tel: +44 (0)1753 833334

Havana House, Bath, 5 Church Street, Abbey Green, Bath, BA1 1NL; Tel: +44 (0)1225 466 197

Havana House, Cardiff (The Bear Shop) 12/14 Wyndham Arcade, Cardiff, CF10 1FJ; Tel: +44 (0)2920 233443

Havana House, Hove, 117 Church Road, Hove, East Sussex, BN3 2AF;
Tel: +44 (0)1273 731 351
Havana House, Oxford, 37 High Street, Oxford, 0X1 4AN;
Tel: +44 (0)1865 243 543
Havana House, Reading, 4 & 5 Harris Arcade, Reading, Berkshire,
RG1 1DN, Tel: +44 (0)118 959 5670
Havana House, Stratford-Upon-Avon, 29 Henley Street,
Stratford-Upon-Avon, CV37 6QN; Tel: +44 (0)1789 292 508

Boisdale - Bishopsgate, Mayfair, Canary Wharf, Belgravia

A quick mention for these bastions of entertaining in a convivial, egalitarian, grown-up way.

Led by my friend and clansman Ranald Macdonald, an inveterate entrepreneur and major cigar lover, each of these Scottish-themed hideaways offers stonking live music, tremendous meat and shellfish, the best wines, thousands of whiskies (and indeed whiskeys) and great humidors bursting with smokes. My favourite terrace is, I think, the one at Belgravia. It's clubbable, but you can be gloriously at peace alone, should you wish. A night at any of these fine establishments is to be looked forward to, savoured and remembered. I recommend you head there – you may well find me, either hosting a cigar event or simply enjoying myself with like-minded cigar folk. Thanks, Ranald.

Acknowledgements

It goes without saying that putting together a book of this scope and navigation can only be achieved with a phenomenal team of friends, contacts, helpers, responders, shoulders to cry on and faithful backers.

To all those who have assisted in my many and varied cigar and travel queries – thank you. Please forgive me if I have forgotten your service; I can assure you, it's not because I do not value it.

Thanks are due, in no particular order, to screen partner in crime, Laurence Davis of Sautter Cigars – thank you for the laughs, the jokes, the drinks, the smokes. Your support, encouragement and not least, your imagination means a lot to me. To my pal Scott Vines from Tor Imports, who's always on the end of the phone or at an airport waiting patiently for me; to Steve Johnstone of Robert Graham, who doesn't get me up to Edinburgh nearly enough but is a great host when he does; to Edward and Eddie Sahakian of Davidoff of London, who treat me like long-lost family and who agreed to provide the foreword to this book – I couldn't be prouder. To Rob and Stuart Fox of J J Fox for free access to their unbounded contacts and their unwavering support – raising a glass to you, lads. To Manu Harit, *mon ami* from The Arts Club. To Darius Namdar of Mark's Club and beyond for his expertise and unfailing generosity.

To Ranald Macdonald for his company and his constant belief in my writing; to Robert Emery for his quiet humour; to Mitchell Orchant of C.Gars

Ltd for his long help and courtesy; to Jemma, Sean and Jimmy from Hunters
& Frankau; to Mirko Pettene of Zechbauer, who believed in this project from
the moment he heard about it; to Kempinski Hotels, which continue to be
the hotels of choice for cigar lovers; to the editorial team at *Cigar Journal*, a
true Band of Brothers; Katja Gnann, who offers her calm help and support
wherever she can; Randy Mastronicola of *Cigar & Spirits* magazine, who
keeps me gainfully occupied with articles for the US cigar market; Matthew,
Sophie and Wesley from London's Oriental Club, which acts like a restor-
ative tonic for this wearied traveller; to Roseanne Cob, for finding Leobo for
me. To Amit Majumdar from Jumeirah Vittaveli for his generous hospitality
in that heavenly place; to Paresh Patel of Havana House for his belief in this
book; to Henke Kelner at Davidoff; Jonathan Drew and Willy Herrera; to
Dr Alejandro Martinez Cuenca, Juan Martínez, Alex Martinez and their
families – as well as the wider family of Joya de Nicaragua – I'll never forget
the trust you placed in me to tell your incredible story.

Thank you Sasja van Horssen for your friendship and no-bullshit support!

Thank you to my family, without whom I wouldn't have had the strength
to begin this journey. And I'd like to dedicate, in part, this book to my friend,
Jeromé Dupont. You are missed.

And finally, thank you to the Sisters, staff and pupils at Belén School in
Estelí, Nicaragua, who taught me that sometimes you have to forget about
yourself to help yourself best.

You are all a part of this project – and you have my gratitude, love
and respect.

About the Author

Nick Hammond has travelled the world in the last twenty-five years, writing for the likes of *Country Life*, *The Daily Telegraph*, *FT How To Spend It*, Fieldsports and many more.

Covering luxury, travel, food and drink – and, of course, cigars – he's also been a newspaper reporter and a copywriter for a blue chip bank. Nick was the inaugural winner of the *Spectator* Cigar Writer of the Year Award and his work is respected worldwide among cigar cognoscenti.

He is also the author of *Cinco Decadas; The Rise of the Nicaraguan Cigar*.

Find out more about RedDoor
Press and sign up to our
newsletter to hear about our
latest releases, author events,
exciting **competitions**
and more at

reddoorpress.co.uk

YOU CAN ALSO FOLLOW US:

     @RedDoorBooks

     Facebook.com/RedDoorPress

     @RedDoorBooks